Beyond the $1 Million Mark

Breaking the Average Barrier

Printed in India

IndiePress

ISBN: 978-93-6045-888-1

First Printing, 2025

IndiePress

A division of Nasadiya Technologies Private Ltd.

Koramangala, Bangalore

Karnataka-560029

http://indiepress.in/

Edited by Literary Connect

Typeset by Pajeflow

Book Cover designed by Sankhasubhro Nath

Publishing Consultant – Samyuktha Prasanan

Contents

Introduction: Why I wrote this 1

We all want something more 5

The feeling stays with us, it does not go away 11

Can we really do it? I think we can! 17

The question is "How?" 41

Changing yourself is not easy 51

Congratulate yourself! *101*

At the end share your success with us 😊 105

One last thing 107

Play to your Strengths 107

Introduction

Why I wrote this

I recently realized I had lost it! 😉

That should hopefully stop you from reading any further. If you do however venture ahead, I can safely say "I told you so'! I warned you.

Have you ever wanted more out of life? Have you ever wondered if there was something you could do that would make your life more amazing than it currently is? Have you ever flirted with the idea of being well known, rich and famous? Have you ever thought about doing something with your life that was so meaningful that it made every moment of your life a memorable journey?

I often have. (I can almost hear the judgment coming down through the pages!) And yet here I am. I don't think I am your average person*. But neither am I successful in any meaningful way. As a measure, I don't think I am known by more than about 1500 people. (The extent of my LinkedIn contacts!).

Let me put it this way, If I popped off tomorrow, apart from my near and dear ones, it wouldn't really matter to anyone in a meaningful way. It wouldn't even create a ripple in the pond of 8 billion lives that inhabit this universe.

** Who is an average person? An average person is a statistical aggregate description of a fictional person who represents the common characteristics or behaviors of most people of a set of people. This fictional person can differ from region to region, by country, by ethnicity, by experience, and by many other factors.*

My most near and dear ones would be devastated, they always are. The Funeral Parlor folks will be happy. My friends and contacts will say "Oh, how sad, can't believe it! That will all get topped off by the few condolence messages on whatever media, my dead soul gets mentioned. And then life will go on. One less person to bother about.

My workplace folks will be shocked! How did this happen??? It's so sad! He was so young! The new job posting will be out in about a week. Soon there will be anywhere between 100 to 200+ applicants depending on whatever the hell I was doing!!! Life goes on, especially in the Corporate World.

It's not that there is a huge difference to this if you are somewhat famous. The shock and consternation are a little larger, maybe lasting for a couple of more days, but then life gets back to normal and everyone goes about their lives.'

I know this is beginning to sound a little gloomy. But I am trying to make a point. So, bear with me.

The point is, nothing I have done till now would cause anyone to remember me. And time is running out as I am on the wrong side of 40. I also want to be remembered in a positive way. I am not wanting to be remembered infamously as a person on the wrong side of the law!

To be fair it wouldn't matter to me once I am dead. So, what I really mean is I want to be doing something or achieving something that would make people sit up and take notice of me *now*. In other words, I want to be successful in this life. I want to have loads of money. I want the good life!

I also read a lot of self-help books and I am always looking at some of the great quotes that keep popping up on all the various media.

"Be grateful for what you have"

I am. I just want more!! (More judgment!)

"Nothing is impossible"

I get the motivational aspect behind this. At the same time if you have tried putting toothpaste back into the tube, after having squeezed it out, you will realize where I am heading with this. Quotes are great. From an absolute technical perspective, they are great. You can actually put toothpaste back into the tube, the only thing is the time and cost to do that would be so prohibitive it wouldn't make sense

This is where I have a problem and this is why I lost it! ☺

I have been trying all this motivational stuff since 2009, that's about 15 years and I am yet to see any earth-shattering results! And that is a long time!

Don't get me wrong. I have had a decent corporate career. I have worked in three different countries spanning across Asia, Europe and the USA. I have had some of the fancy designations of Vice President, Director etc. I have traveled the World. I have the right of residency in more than one Country. I have a wonderful family. And yet, for some reason I want more!!

So, either I have lost it. (Which I mentioned earlier!) Or "we" are onto something!

The "we" here is all you readers and me.

This is the point where you either say you are happy where you are. Or you set out on a journey with me to see where it takes us.

This is why I wrote this book.

Only those who think they want something more out of life need to go ahead with reading this. The other warning, I want to give everyone is this. I have still not figured anything out. I have no @#$%&@# clue of how I am going to get what I want. I have no idea of how I can get to a place where I think "yes" I have got what I wanted! The only thing I do know is that through my ramblings over the next few chapters I am going to experiment with some possible paths. After all, there is never any harm in trying.

So, let's get started on the next few chapters of "Beyond the $1 Million Mark" and see where it takes us!

I do want to make a point here. I actually wrote all this myself. It's not written by any of the AI software out there. It's truly me. I must say I am impressed with AI's ability to write stuff, and I am sure it will soon become the norm, but at least for this book, it's all me. Whether for good or for bad!

***

We all want something more

It's strange how I have struggled with this feeling for so long. Ever since I was a kid, I have always wanted something more in life. For some strange reason, life got in the way. Or perhaps it was me who got in the way. It was probably me. I am a firm believer in blaming no one but myself.

I agree we are responsible for everything we are. We can't really blame anyone except ourselves. And I get that. My problem is I still want something more out of life. And a lot of those things seem to be the same things I wanted when I was much younger and didn't have the courage to go after.

And that's where being just above average comes into play, I guess. I was slightly better than some of my classmates at studying, and hence ended up in a half decent educational institution, after which it was pretty much like a sausage factory line up. Study, get a job, work hard, earn money, marry, have children, etc. etc. Again, not a bad life, in fact it's been an amazing journey so far. And yet I still seem to want something more.

I am also convinced that if you are *still* reading this, then you are probably in the same boat.

We all want something more.

Just to complicate things a little more, (and I like doing that!) there are two different ways in which we want something more.

One is where we have achieved a level of success in what we are doing and what we like doing. For example, you are a successful musician, or a very successful Business person, or a successful athlete, and you want to be even more successful. Wanting that is natural human behavior. We always want to improve on where we are. It's evolution. It's what drives the World and leads to successive generations of improvement in everything we do.

If you are in this category, as in you are doing what you love and you are reasonably successful, then you are pretty blessed. Keep moving ahead and you will probably find what you are looking for. I am sure there will be challenges and sometimes you will feel as if you are stagnating or perhaps not being as successful as you would like to be, but that is natural. There is a good chance you will eventually reach where you want to be.

A number of us are however in that second category of people who are stuck doing something that pays the bills! We are reasonably good at what we do, we are making a decent living, but we want something more or most likely something different in life.

If for some reason you are in this category, then there is another thing I will share with you as well. It's both an inspirational and an irritating thing depending on what mood you are in. It's the saying below.

"Do what you love doing and you won't have to work another day in your life." Or some variant of this. I won't even bother to try and tell you who said this and so on. Time is too short. The point is it's easier said than done!

Yeah, I love reading books! How will doing that all day make me money? Or I love trekking, or hiking, or biking, or music, or even writing. But how is that going to help me make a living? Starting small, doing it on the side, is obviously one of the solutions, and a number of people have tried it and some have been very successful. They are the ones you might have probably heard about.

I am not one of them. (Did I just hear "loser?" You could be right!) And hence I am trying to figure things out as I suspect you are as well.

Figuring out what we want is not as simple as it sounds. I am a great believer in brevity, less is more etc. but I don't think it applies to the problem at hand. I don't think this is something that can be solved with a tweet or an Instagram post.

I probably lost most of you there!

The challenge we face is something like this. Let's assume for a moment, I love painting. I can paint for a few hours and during that time I can forget the World around me and just immerse myself in it. So, I keep painting. I churn out quite a few paintings. The problem is I am a slightly above average painter, but I am not particularly talented. I make a series, set up an exhibition, sell a few paintings, (all whilst working at whatever pays my bills!), and then realize that the effort is not commensurate with the earnings. I realize I am making more money from the job I don't like than making the paintings I love doing. Sure, it gets me some money, but it's not getting me the big money. Perhaps later it will, but in the immediate future it won't.

The obvious solution seems to be to keep slugging away and not letting go. But then the other thing I had mentioned earlier is a factor as well. And that is the fact that I am not particularly talented when it comes to painting. I may like it, I may love it, but I am not greatly talented. There are many more people out there who are much more talented than me and a number of them are struggling as well. So how do I reconcile this? As I mentioned at the beginning of the paragraph, tenacity. Tenacity seems to be one of the hallmarks of success. We have all heard about it and yes, it is one of the solutions that can help us be successful. The thing is a number of us are unable to keep up that level of tenacity in conjunction with a job that pays our bills. Or it could even simply be that we don't have that level of commitment.

So, what next for that budding painter within me, or for that matter, within you? Does it peter out, or do I keep going? Perhaps if I keep going, someday someone might notice my paintings and take an interest in helping me promote it. Would that then be a case of a bit of well-deserved luck, since I have been slaving away at my passion? Possibly yes.

So now there are three things at play here. A love of doing something. An ability to stick with it. And finally, a bit of luck. So, if it is really that simple, why haven't we, who are still reading, including myself, not reached where we want to be? It's because each one of these three things have deeper nuances to them. For example, do you really love the act of painting itself? Or do we love the feeling we get when we are painting? Or do we love the part where we conceptualize a painting? Or do we love the fact that people appreciate our paintings? Or is it a combination of two or more of these? How long can we sustain these feelings in order to have a remarkable output? How do we define tenacity? When does tenacity turn to drudgery and start affecting output? And so, it goes on.

The point is, whilst we may all want something more, figuring out what exactly we want is sometimes the first step. And it's different for all of us. Some of us may like surfing the waves, some of us may like flying, some of us may like playing a game, some of us may like doing advanced research, and some of us may like politics. There is no end to the things we may like doing. It's also not necessary we only like one thing. We may like multiple things. A lot of us do. For example, I may like writing and traveling. Some may like surfing and skateboarding and gaming. Someone may like bird watching, music and martial arts.

It's important to remind everyone here as well, that what we are talking about here is we want something more out of life. I did steer the conversation here to make it seem as if one of the key ways to get there is to do something you like or love doing. It definitely is, but you could also get something more out of life whilst doing something you don't love so much. It has happened with people, so let's not rule that out as well.

An example of that could be you are doing very well at your job. It's probably not your first love, but you are doing well. What you really love however is traveling to different parts of the World. And because of the kind of job, you have you are able to do that. So, in a way you have got a bit of what you want out of life.

But then we come back to the original issue of "we still want something more."

Again, a lot of what I have rambled on about is both contextual and relative to each one of us as an individual. Each one of us will perceive our own need for something more, differently. It will be tailored to our own specific wants and desires. For example, there may be two people who like to travel. At the same time, one of them loves traveling by air, whilst the other prefers taking Cruises. Then there are people who probably prefer traveling by road.

I think I am beginning to lose the point I am trying to make! (I never said I was a writer!)

I guess what I am trying to say is as below:

Deep down within all of us there is always a desire to want something more than what we have. To my mind it is a good thing. It constantly forces us to try and grow and improve. In fact, that is probably the engine of the World which drives the evolution and progress we see around us.

So, in my mind I have established the fact that we all seem to want something more out of life. Again, according to me it is a good thing. The thing I grapple with is how to get the "something more" that I want out of life. How do I make it a reality? Especially when I sometimes feel I may have already missed the bus.

But before we go there, I also wanted to explore the concept of giving up these desires. After all, can't we be happy with what we have. Why do we really need to hanker after more?

Let's explore that concept in our next chapter!

***

The feeling stays with us, it does not go away

Throughout the last many years, I have often told myself about how grateful I am for what I have. I truly am. I have a blessed life. A few challenges here and there, but I still consider myself blessed.

Yet there is something within me that keeps bubbling up from time to time that says "go out there and give it a shot."

Yeah, I hear voices in my head!! I did tell you I had lost it right in the beginning. You still chose to stay with me!

It comes up on you or rather creeps up on you in two ways. The first way is when you are watching something or reading something. You see, hear or read something that reminds you of what your dreams were. You see something and think "I could have been easily doing that! And I could probably do it better!"

Or you see something and wish you either had what they were showing or experiencing what they were showing. An example is the picture below.

When I see something like this I always wonder for a moment. I wish I could have my own yacht and could sail into the deep blue ocean with not a worry in the World. I wish I didn't have to bother about money, or the need to get back to a job or anything of that nature. I would sip champagne, nibble on caviar and listen to the music I love with not a care in the World. (I would probably nibble on a packet of chips. I haven't really tasted caviar properly yet. You get the drift though!)

Bottomline, I want to have a good time! Some people have cautioned me I would get bored of all this soon. That soon I would get used to all that and would then wonder what to do. Maybe I would and maybe I wouldn't but the point is I want to find out for myself? Don't you?

If you do, you will also identify with what I will talk about next.

You are watching this intense movie. The protagonist goes through a series of challenges but then is able to overcome all of them and be wildly successful in what he, or she, or they end up doing. You can recall your own favorite movie and as you recall the music rising to a crescendo as the protagonist finally emerges successful, you might recall a sense of nostalgia that would have crept up on you. Maybe that could have been you! Yes, it could have been. And you wonder what life would have been like.

We don't really talk about these moments to anyone. Sometimes we don't even tell our near and dear ones, because even to ourselves it seems silly or far-fetched or out of reach. It sure does and it probably may be, but the point is we still want something more. It has not gone away from us. It sits there somewhere in that thing we call a brain, and it rears itself up from time to time in an attempt to push us out of our comfort zone.

But then it mostly dies down. Monday comes along and we are back at the daily grind of life, with our dreams tucked away at the back of our minds. For me it gets tucked away, but of late it seems to pop out more often. It just doesn't want to go away. Perhaps that is why I say I have lost it!

The point I am trying to make here is this feeling of wanting something more out of life does not seem to go away. It just keeps coming back. And the biggest question I face, or rather we face, since you are obviously still reading, is, what do we do?

How do we tackle this? How do we do something that gets us to where we want to be? Is there really a way? Or are we destined to this intermittent nostalgia about how things might have been?

Maybe we are. There have been times when I have thought to myself. "Look, you really have missed the bus, at least in this lifetime. And if you really want to be that star athlete, or that great scientist, or that great writer, or that great singer, or that great politician, you will have to wait for your next life, if there is one!"

I guess I need to take the politician bit back!

The above thinking works for a bit. But then again, the thought of doing something in this lifetime, doing something now, rears its annoying head, and I find myself back to square one. That is wanting something more out of life! More out of this life. Right here, right now!

That is why I say it never really goes away. We all still want something more out of life.

The internet has been a boon to some of us. I often see people whom I knew in school, or college, or at work, posting things about what they are doing, or posting videos in which they are doing something they have always wanted to do. Social media is a great tool for people to try out new things. Admittedly it's an overcrowded space, but nevertheless it's there. And people are using it to become famous, and in some cases famous overnight, when something goes viral.

One of the reasons I think we all want to do something more, or get something more out of life, is because of our innate need for recognition or appreciation. Somewhere deep down we do want people to appreciate us or like us. We are ready to do the hard work, we are ready to put in the hours that are needed, but at the end we need genuine appreciation. Our souls crave it, whether or not we acknowledge it.

I will digress here for a moment. For those of us in the Corporate World, you will often hear about how it's important to recognize and appreciate employees. Some big organizations have actually made it into a formal tool, with reminders being sent to managers, to appreciate their people. I bring this up for two reasons.

The first reason is to demonstrate that recognition or appreciation is one of the most important things we all crave. If the Corporate world has woken up to it after so much research, then it's probably true. The fact they screw it up most of the time is a different issue.

The second reason I bring it up, is that if you have ever been on the receiving end of such corporate appreciation, there is a 50% chance it does not quite give you the satisfaction you crave. I am sure it does in some cases, but in a lot of cases it does not. Furthermore, you are probably craving that recognition and appreciation in a field that is outside the Corporate World in the field or hobby that you are interested in, and yet cannot pursue. It's like a thirst that can never be slaked. (I am feeling like a Vampire now! One that refrains from human blood!)

I had read somewhere that human beings actually need appreciation more than they need food. At the same time, whilst it's easy to admit the need for food, it's an accepted fact, we find it very difficult to acknowledge that we need appreciation. And without appreciation they say the "soul withers away."

Now this is not a spiel about appreciation. It's about how "the appreciation" that we crave for deep down within ourselves, is probably a by-product of the "something more" we want out of life.

We know deep down that once we have achieved something more in our life, once we have gone out and cracked it, universal appreciation will follow. Again, for some of us this may not seem true, and so be it. It's just one of the many possibilities of why our need for "something more" does not seem to go away.

As I said "the feeling" stays with us and it refuses to go away.

I once met a person who by every means was very successful in her Corporate Life. She had everything you could ask for, a great job, she was good at it and had a great standing in the industry, a great family, a beautiful house, and yet she wanted something more. I could see it in her eyes as we had that drink together. She wanted something more. She wanted to follow her real passion that she had put aside all these years whilst climbing the corporate ladder.

Her words to me were as follows;

"I spent a good number of years getting here and now I am going to spend the rest of my time trying out this new thing! And you know what, I don't even care if I am successful or not. I just want to do it."

I happen to know she went on to do very well at what she chose to do and right now is very successful at what she set out to do. I am not sure whether or not she has satisfied her need for something more, but I am hoping to get a chance to ask her in the near future.

Coming back to the topic, and more importantly if you are still with me on this journey, then the conclusion is as below:

Whatever the reason, our quest for something more remains with us whether we like it or not. And it keeps rearing its head up and down, precisely because it has never really gone away from our minds. And that is why you and I are on this journey to find out whether or not we can find that "something more" we crave for.

***

Can we really do it? I think we can!

A lot of people including myself have no doubt asked this question. Can we really go after that "something more" we want out of life? Or is it just something we all need to live with. Is it just reserved for those few courageous, supremely gifted or talented, rich, lucky or destined people to get what they want? Or can we the "Neither Average Nor Successful" population aspire for that elusive "something more" I have been writing about.

If you have been putting up with me till now, you are probably in that 20% of readers who are still with me. 80% of the readers have already abandoned me or rather us, by now. I inserted this piece of information after one of my possible publishers told me 80% of the people who would read this would not like it!

I decided to be tenacious for a change.

Whether we can do it or not will be directly proportional to the extent of our feelings for what we really want. If we really feel about something strongly, we will be able to find a way to get there. As an example, I will share a small story about something I tried with some level of success, a couple of times.

In 2010 I decided I wanted to experience Asia in the form of either Hong Kong or Singapore. I was based out of Mumbai at the time. I started thinking about it. I started talking about it. I would talk about it to everyone I met, my colleagues, my friends, my acquaintances and even someone I would have met at the bar. One of my colleagues once said to me, he was amazed at how I brought up this subject with one of our contractors at a site meeting. I was equally surprised because I must have done it as a habit, and didn't even remember the exact details of what I must have said. The point was I would constantly think about it, talk about it and work towards it.

I started looking for jobs in both Singapore and Hong Kong. I started getting in touch with placement agents in Hong Kong, and I remember one lady who was so encouraging, that I actually ended up traveling to Hong Kong and meeting her. I did not get a job through her, and I think it's important to mention I didn't get any future jobs through her, but what I do remember is her encouragement at a time like that, did more for me than a lot of other things I had tried.

It may sound strange, but I started looking at some of the beautiful pictures of both Singapore and Hong Kong. I looked at images of the skylines by day and by night and kept visualizing myself reaching there. I even started keeping my computer passwords as Singapore12 or HongKong12, as we had to change passwords every three months!

The net result was, I started a new job in Hong Kong in February, 2012. It took me one and half years to get what I wanted. But I got it. And I got it by constantly thinking about it. By constantly focusing on it.

The above is borne out by two other people who I personally know in the corporate World, one of whom has moved from Australia to the US and the other from Europe to the US. I will not reveal who they are for privacy reasons, but based on my discussions with them at various times, I realized they were following the same process as above, albeit in their own way.

It's also important to take the opportunity you get even if it's not perfect. It all works out in the end. The first job I had been offered when I was moving to Hong Kong, was not perfect. I said yes, I was happy to take it. A few days later the job itself got canceled due to budget constraints. At the same time the person who was doing a part of that job resigned and they offered his role to me. I took it and it turned out to be one of the best decisions of my life. In three years, I ended up becoming the Region Head for Asia Pacific based out of Hong Kong. I actually became my boss's boss! It would never have happened if I had continued to stay where I was. And boy, did I enjoy my years in Asia in Hong Kong! I wasn't too enamored with my job. It paid the bills and it was hard work. So, my thinking was, I probably have to work hard anyway for a living, so why not see the World whilst doing it. I traveled to so many parts of Asia, including 10 Cities in China, Taiwan, Korea, Japan, Malaysia, Singapore, Vietnam, Australia, Philippines, Indonesia, you name it! And everywhere I tried to experience the culture, the people, the food and everything that a new place had to offer. It was something I had always dreamed of doing and I got to do it.

4 years later I wanted to move out of Hong Kong and I set my sights on either the US or the UK. I wanted to gain some experience working in one of these Countries and also see more of the World. Again, I started thinking about it, talking to people, looking for opportunities. One of the things I had learnt by then, was whilst it's important to look for opportunities outside of your current organization, it is easier to move abroad within your existing organization. So, this time I focused more on working through the internal channels. Again, the process took time. It was close to a year and a half before I managed to move to the US with my family. At the same time, I followed the same steps I have outlined earlier. I thought about where I wanted to move. I looked up travel books for the US. I looked at pictures of New York and London. I created passwords which said New York 12 or London 12.

I finally got an opportunity to move to the US, not to New York, but to another City. It was a lateral move. I was not getting a big raise or anything. But I was getting what I wanted and I took the opportunity.

I moved to the US in 2017. When I look back 7 years from now, I think it was one of the best things I ever did. This time I got to go newer places, some of them being, Mexico, Argentina, Costa Rica, Brazil, Canada, Colombia, Moscow, Poland, Dublin, Italy, Hungary and Sweden. All such wonderful places! I also got a chance to get around North America, including New York, Boston, LA, San Francisco, Chicago, Washington, Atlanta, Las Vegas, Ithaca, Arizona, Minneapolis and Indianapolis. And I am still in the process of visiting more places!

To summarize, I thought about what I wanted and took the appropriate actions to help materialize the same. I also made the best of the opportunities I got. I took them!

It made me realize if you really want something, you can make it happen, up to a certain extent. Again, whilst it didn't get me what I *really* wanted; it got me some parts of it. I wanted to see the World and I was able to do that and do that in style!

Another thing I notice with people, is whilst they may be doing something they don't really like, they keep going back to what they really love, in their spare time.

There is this woman I know who does fabulous paintings. I would think she probably paints better than some commercial artists I have seen. But the Corporate World pays her better to keep doing what she does, and therefore she does not paint full time. At the same time, she does return to her paintings whenever she gets some time and that keeps her balanced.

Some of us may have already identified something we would like to do and are waiting for the right moment. For some people that often happens after retirement or if they end up leaving their job, or even losing their job.

There are also some of us, who know we want something more, but we haven't really identified what that is. Some of us are in a state where we could suddenly find ourselves with tons and tons of money, without the need to work, and yet we would struggle to figure out what it is we want to do. We would know we want something more, but we still have to go through the journey of finding out what exactly we want. And that is perfectly fine. Every person starts his or her or their journey at a different point. The intention is to figure out how we can get to that "something more" we want out of life.

The more I dabble with this idea, the more I get convinced we can actually do it. We can find out what we want and we can find a way to be wildly successful in what we want.

It will take an effort on our part though. But it is an effort all of us who are reading this are capable of. Remember I started out saying, we are above average. So, it's not that we have not worked hard. We have. We have spent years in the grind. So yes, we are ready to put in the effort. All we need is someone to help us get pointed in the right direction and then stick with it.

Yeah, sounds simple, but it obviously isn't, else each one of us would have been counting our blessings, spending our Millions, and definitely not reading this book!

The thing however is I am convinced it can be done. I am not going to try and share success stories of countless people here. If any of you have been reading till now, you have probably heard of the success stories of countless successful people who had to struggle in the early part of their lives, or whatever. Yeah, you have seen that and heard that. We are talking about ourselves here. We are in a different boat. We are not successful right now, or at least not successful in the way we want to be. Remember the title of the book? "Beyond the $1 Million Mark."

So, hearing about how Arnold Schwarzenegger made it, or how Obama overcame all odds, or how Sharukh Khan made it big, is not going to help us at this stage. We have either read or heard all that before.

What we are really looking for is something else. We are looking to see how we can move out of our average life to a wildly successful life. We are not looking to do something drastic such as quitting our jobs tomorrow and venturing out into some wildly unsuccessful venture which we love, but gets us next to nothing in earnings. We are looking for that elusive way to success, a success that is defined by us, within a finite amount of time, without disrupting our status quo of a lifestyle.

There, I think I have come to some sort of a definition of what we want.

"We are looking for a way to success, a success that is defined by us, within a finite amount of time, without disrupting our status quo of a lifestyle."

Let me know if you agree with this. You can do this by shooting an email to dreamsellers12@gmail.com. Yeah, that's an email I use to pick up feedback. A lot of it is about folks telling me to stop writing! But you may think differently.

Coming back to where we were.

If you do agree with the above, the question is "can we really do it?" I think we can and hence this book. I sincerely think we can. This is not where I say, I have done it and hence you can. Neither do I say others have done it and hence you can. What I say is *it's worth a try. And if it's worth a try then there is a way it can be done. All we have to do is find it.*

I am still looking for it. And that's the journey I will take you on. A journey led simply by a belief we can be wildly successful in the time that is left to us.

I am going to digress here a bit. I am going to bring in the concept of belief here for a bit. After all I am allowed to go in different directions, given, I am not your traditional writer.

Belief is probably one of the most important things we will need to address as we go along on this journey. And I am going to try and introduce the concept of belief through a very different subject here. It's a subject I have explored a bit, but more importantly it allows me to demonstrate how it's so hard to change our beliefs. And sometimes we may need to do that a little as we try to become successful.

The subject I am going talk about here is "longevity." It's one of those futuristic things that have the Jeff Bezos and Elon Musk's of the World all excited about. It's probably the "something more" they are looking for!

I have been thinking and reading about longevity, life extension, immortality, reverse aging and the like for the past many years. As mentioned earlier, I have also traveled quite extensively during that time, and every time I traveled, be it to Seoul in Korea, or Buenos Aires in Argentina, or Cities including Mexico, Moscow, Hong Kong, New York and London, I would ask the people I met there about these concepts.

The reason I would do so was to get an idea about what people tend to think or believe about life. I would set it up something like this.

Usually after a few rounds of drinks and dinner we would be finishing the last round of drinks with the conversation beginning to taper off. I would then start off by pointing to a glass of liquid, it could be water, it could be a leftover drink, it didn't matter, and pose the following questions to the group. Usually about six to seven people.

"Let's for a moment imagine this liquid is the nectar of immortality." That usually gets people's attention. "If you were to drink this you would live forever." I would clarify that people could not ask me counter questions and they had to answer yes or no.

It does take a bit of time to get things going but once I laid the ground rules, I would begin to get answers. Usually, the first round of questioning would elicit an answer of mostly "no." Sometimes one or at most two people would say "yes."

I would then reframe the question to say, "If you were to drink this not only would you live forever, but you could also share it with your family and friends." This round sometimes would get an additional "yes" response.

The next round is crucial. My question would be as below:

"If you were to drink this not only would you live forever, you would do so in the physical condition you were at 25 *and* you could also share it with your family and friends."

At this point you start getting an additional "yes." And whilst you see there are still quite a few "no's'" you can sense people are thinking about the concept.

I then throw in the fact you will also have a choice, that were you to get bored with life for some reason, after say 150 or 200 years, you could choose to opt for a painless death.

As you would have guessed all of this does lead to a lively discussion, especially since everyone has had a few drinks!

It will be interesting to note that by the end of these interactions I would usually have about 50% of the audience in the "yes" category. That is a significant statistic, for me, especially considering this exercise is done over about 15 to 20 minutes and people aren't obviously taking it seriously. What it has led me to believe though is that there is a "strong level of interest" in this concept. Another thing I also noticed is that people towards the "so called older side" of the spectrum were more likely to say "yes."

This exercise also leads to some interesting questions and I am going to talk about each one of them here. The reason is each one of these questions really arise from our present concept of life, our current beliefs, the way it has been taught to us, and the way we have seen it unfold before us till now. Our belief system plays a very important part in how we view life. All our concepts of life are a combination of what we have seen till now, what we have heard and what our religious beliefs tell us. We are all right in our own way.

My approach has always been "can we possibly look at things a little differently?"

One of the first and foremost questions that come up with regard to longevity is as below:

Is it ethical or right for us to try and prolong life?

It is a very valid question. For many years I too had the belief we should not meddle with what nature has provided us. As time progressed however, I realized that with advances in medicine and science, we were actually averting death for millions of people across the World. We were treating all types of diseases, including cancer, which a mere 100 years ago would been a death sentence for most people. We were extending life for a number of people by at least a decade if not more.

We are doing this today with advancements in the medical field and it is an accepted fact of life. Let me take an example. If one of our loved ones at 80 years needed a lifesaving surgery, would I not get it done? If I was told that it would let that person live for another 10 years, would I not get it done? I would imagine most of us would.

The way I look at it, it is acceptable for us to prolong life into the 80's and 90's, but we are not sure it's ethical to go too much beyond that. I get it. And this is where our beliefs come in. We currently tend to hold the following belief:

Humans can live healthy lives up to say about 80 or 90 after which they will probably succumb to some illness and pass away. That is the cycle of life and that is the way it should be.

We all know there are outliers to the above with some people living beyond 100 etc. but we view them as outliers as well.

I am now going to try and approach this question slightly differently based on what we know and believe today.

Let's assume for a moment that the human lifespan was only 40 years. Let's assume from the moment we were born we were led to believe we would only live for a maximum of 40 years, with the occasional outlier going up to 45. Everything we would see around us would provide us evidence of that fact. People would actually die from old age at around 40, some earlier and some later. All around us we would see people pacing their lives, knowing that 40 was the expected life expectancy.

People would probably start working at an earlier age, get married at an earlier age, have children etc. by their mid to late teens. People would probably work till their early to mid-thirties and then lead a retired life in their late thirties. It's important to note that our bodies would also mature and grow faster were this to be the case. Given the fact the current life expectancy is around 80, a life expectancy of around 40 would essentially mean that everything that happens to us during a year of our lives, would happen to us in 6 months. So, in effect a 5-year-old with a life expectancy of 40 would be as old as a 10-year-old of the present-day scenario, with a life expectancy of 80.

If for centuries the above would have been the case, we would have accepted that fact and that would have been our reality. Our whole lives would have been designed around the life expectancy of 40 years. Everything from schools, to colleges, to jobs, to marriages, to healthcare and retirement would be designed around that time frame. Anyone who then lives up to an age of 50 would be an absolute outlier and would find a place in the Guinness book of World Records.

I know it's difficult to imagine the above scenario. But let's try and imagine that it is true. Let's try to put ourselves into a society where we all believe that the maximum life expectancy for a normal person is 40.

Try as you might, it's not easy to do that. At the back of your mind, you will find it really difficult to do that. I can see you thinking. " This is a hypothetical exercise." "We all know that the real-life expectancy today is around 80, So why would I think that it would ever be 40." And I agree with you. It is extremely difficult and, in some cases, almost impossible to change our beliefs. So, let's try and look at this in a different way.

Let's assume you come across a totally isolated society that has managed to live hidden from the rest of mankind for centuries. Let's imagine this society is discovered and after a lot of initial euphoria it slowly begins to start integrating with our society. We also discover this society has an average life expectancy of 40 years.

As medical experts interact with this new society, they discover there is a reason they only have a life expectancy till 40. It is due to a certain genetic modification that had happened a long time ago. The good news is it is easy to correct and with a few years of treatment, they could actually get everyone to live healthy lives till 80, just the way we do. There is a lot of excitement about this discovery and the initial expectation is a lot of people would embrace this opportunity to extend their life span to 80 years.

However, it's not quite easily accepted by this society. There is a reason for that. For centuries their beliefs have been molded by a life expectancy for 40 years. Their entire lifestyle, their religious beliefs, everything is centered around a 40-year lifespan. The question they ask themselves is as follows:

Is it ethical or right for us to try and prolong life?

From the perspective of our medical fraternity, it had initially seemed like a no brainer. Why wouldn't they want it? But as they find out, there are fewer takers of the treatment than they thought.

What would seem ethical and right from our point of view (we who are used to living till 80), would not seem right to someone, who has only been used to seeing and believing that the maximum they should be living life to was around 40. For them to try and prolong life till 80 would be like trying to play God. It would seem like they were doing something that was interfering with the normal way of life. We however from our point of view would think it perfectly normal for them to take the treatment and go on to live a full life up to 80 or beyond.

No one here is right or wrong. It's about looking at things from different perspectives. Sometimes these different perspectives are needed in order for us to become wildly successful.

Let us now look at a different scenario. Let us imagine we come across another hidden society which has remained hidden from us for centuries, a lot like the previous society I mentioned. Only in this case we realize they have life spans going up to 160 years!!

Turns out now that our society just needs a few genetic modifications this time, and with a few years of treatment, we too could live healthy lives up to an age of 160. Essentially, we would end up doubling our healthy lifespan.

Would we embrace it? Would we, do it?

My answer to this has always been "We don't really know and it will take time."

It will take time for most people to embrace such concepts. Over a period of time as more and more people start adopting these changes it will become more accepted and over a period of 20 to 30 years people may slowly adapt.

If you have been reading till here, then I would like to take a moment here to thank you. The reason I do that is because of your patience with me. As I started to write about this topic, I realized it is a topic that raises multiple questions at every stage. I realize that everything I have written above raises further questions and thoughts in the reader's mind. For example, there will be questions around feasibility. There will be questions around religious beliefs and ethics. There will be questions around finances, resources, etc. etc.

I will try my best to address and answer some of these questions, but I also realize that try as I might I will not be able to address every question that will come up. But I will try since what I am doing here is showing you the layers of beliefs, we all carry with respect to just one hypothetical topic. In the meantime, I will thank you once again for going on this journey with me and I will try and answer the second most asked question when it comes to living longer, which is as below:

Will we be healthy as we prolong life?

This is one of the most important questions I face as I continue to explore these ideas.

Do you know what is "Gerascophobia?"

It is the fear of getting old. For some people getting old can be scary. There are ways to manage this fear but one of the key reasons why people have this fear is because they associate old age with a loss of independence. Loss of independence is probably the biggest fear people have as they are growing old. In fact, for some, this is greater than the fear of death. There is a good reason for this fear.

Nobody wants to be dependent on someone else for their needs, especially since before they became old, they have been used to being independent. This association of "ill health" with living longer is one of the main reasons people balk at wanting to live a longer life.

Therefore, the question: Can we live a longer life and at the same time be *healthy and independent*?

All the research that is happening around this subject is focusing on exactly this question. People generally don't want to live longer with a body that is failing. If the body is healthy and the mind is functioning, then it is a different matter altogether. That is what all the companies and research labs in this area are focusing on.

In short, they are looking to "reverse the effects of aging." They are treating ageing as the "issue" that needs to be treated. Once they are able to do that, the belief is, people will be able to live longer and healthier lives.

One of the key reasons we age is because of our "Telomeres" getting shorter as time goes by. "Telomeres" are an integral part of the millions of cells that our bodies are made of. They essentially affect how our cells age. Telomeres act like caps at the end of each stretch of DNA, within our cells, that protect our chromosomes.

An easy way to visualize a telomere is to think about it like a plastic tip at the end of our shoelace. With time as this plastic tip gets damaged the ends of the shoelaces become frayed and we are unable to use them.

Similarly, our DNA strands get damaged and can't do their job, which in turn affects the ability of our cells to divide.

In short, as we lose the telomeres our cells age and die.

This has been known to us for a long time and there are studies happening all around the World to see how we can prolong the life of telomeres. There is a race amongst scientists globally to solve this aspect of aging along with many other aspects of the aging process.

The point I am making here is there is research going on to reach a point where the human life can be extended whilst having a healthy body. Having a healthy body is key to life extension. Nobody wants to be living to 120 with an aging body that keeps having one illness after the other. If, however your body feels the way it was when you were in your 20's or 30's, or even 40s you probably wouldn't mind living a little longer.

There are various other factors involved with aging and there is research happening around all these aspects. It's not going to be easy, but it is happening, and it will continue to happen. If you google this subject, you will find thousands of articles that talk about this. You will also find various longevity diets and pills on the market as well, all of which are aimed at life extension. It is the next frontier that people are trying to reach.

It's interesting how during one of my discussions with a friend on this subject, he articulated what he thought would happen. He essentially outlined what would happen in his lifetime.

According to him, he thought that when he reached about 70, science would have figured out a way to keep him alive for another 20 years in reasonable health. 20 years is a long time. At the end of that 20 years, he reckoned they would have figured out how to get him an additional 30 years in reasonable health. If you do the math, that brings him to 120 years of age. By then he thought they would have probably discovered a way to not only extend life but even perhaps reverse aging altogether. The point was he thought he would see this happen incrementally over our lifetime, whilst future generations would probably be born to a World where living up to 150 or 200 years was normal.

I had quite liked his hypothesis and therefore I have shared it here. I think it is quite valid, and it answers the question I had posed earlier.

Will we be healthy as we prolong life?

I think for our generation we will be reasonably healthy, as we prolong our life in increments, with a very good chance of our health improving as we age, given the new discoveries around reverse aging. Our future generations will obviously have it much better. At the same time, I would consider our generation as possibly one of the luckiest and most fortunate generations to be alive at a time like this, on the cusp of all these major discoveries.

Am I beginning to challenge your beliefs? Think about how you feel as you consider these ideas. It does not matter whether you think this will happen or not. Focus on how you feel. Try and understand how we resist things that are contrary to what we have come to believe. It's important, because one of the paths to becoming successful, is to challenge traditional beliefs.

Coming back to longevity. One of the other questions I often face when I discuss this topic relates to the question as below:

The World is already over populated with people. If people started living longer there would be no space for them on earth! Or, we would run out of resources!

A very relevant question, and it's worthwhile to examine this a little further.

The population of the World in 1930 was 2 billion

Today it is almost 8 billion

It will most likely peak at around 2070 at 9.4 billion.

The above is assuming that no one extends their life. After this point the population will start declining and by 2100 a mere 30 years later it will decline to 9 billion. (i.e., it will actually go down by 400 million people!)

If people were to opt for a longer life of about 200 years, this is about the time the whole process would begin to kick in, in real earnest. Again, we have to understand that everyone will not opt for this life elongation at first. So, it will be a slower process, before the numbers start going up.

We also have to be cognizant of the fact that as more and more people opt for these strategies there will be a change in people's behaviors. For example, people may opt to have children at much later ages. With advances in science and technology having children at a later age will be much more feasible than it is now.

Let's take an example of what the child bearing age was historically. According to some statistics I picked off the internet, in the 1920's people were having kids in their twenties. A hundred years later people are normally having kids in their late twenties. That is about a 5-year shift. So given medical advances it's not unlikely that this will shift even further upwards.

The bottom line is that whilst there will be an impact on population it will not be a significant one and it will be manageable at a Global level. It is also important to remember two other relevant facts.

What we are talking about will only start happening at a more rapid pace and more universally after about 20 to 40 years. That is a lot of time.

The second important thing we need to think about is what else would be happening during those 20 to 40 years with respect to the universe. What would be happening with respect to human beings moving to the Moon or Mars? Would there be intermittent populations living in large space stations? Would we be exploring life under the oceans? Whilst it all seems a little fantastic, it's not really beyond the realms of possibility.

Let me now share an interesting statistic. 57% of the current World's land area is uninhabited at this point. Even if we were to populate a small percentage of this area on earth, we would have enough space for a few million more people. Compared to space, the moon and Mars, it is a much more easily achievable venture. Yes, it will take advances in technology and a sustainable approach, but it is possible.

What I am saying is with the exponential growth of technology and with our reliance on the ingenuity of the human mind, we will find a sustainable way to manage the increase in population that extended longevity will bring about. At the very least it will not bring about the doom and gloom we think it will.

I am aware a lot of us may not buy into these arguments and I respect that. As I mentioned at the beginning, for some of us this concept of increasing our healthy lifespan may seem untenable or undesirable at this point. I would say it is a perfectly acceptable point of view and I think it will act as a great check on the population growth as well, since a lot of people will not buy into these concepts at all. As a result, in the end state there will be space for all to thrive.

The reason though I bring it up is important. Think about how you feel as you start thinking about this idea. Forget about what you have heard from people. For a moment let go of any limiting beliefs you might have and just toy around with the concept. For some of you this may be easy. You may just embrace it. For some it may sound interesting, as something that others may do, but you wouldn't. Some may even find it abhorrent or blasphemous. And that is perfectly fine. The point is, it's important for us to understand our beliefs and how deep rooted they are with respect to any subject. It will have a bearing on whether we are successful or not.

The next question I often get is how will we finance our longevity?

A great question!! And probably one of the most important ones.

How will we have the money to live for an additional 100 or 120 years? Where will it come from? What sort of savings will we need? Will we have to keep working longer? What sort of jobs will we get? What sort of insurances will cover us?

Let me detract here for a bit.

If we look back at history, we will see that all the great explorers, discoverers, and adventurists, they all took risks. They took risks with their lives and many of them actually died trying to discover something new. Most of them did not know what lay in store for them ahead. Yet they went ahead and tried. Some of them were pioneers, some became famous and yes, some of them died. The point is it did not stop them.

Any of us who embark on a journey of deliberately increasing our lifespan in this generation will face risks. The risks will not just be Financial. There will be other risks as well. There will be social risks, there will be risks of feeling isolated, there will be risks of botched medical procedures, risks of accidents etc. Yet those of us who do decide to take these risks will find a way to face them.

As we find the courage and means to face these risks, we will also find ways to finance our own longevity.

One of the things we will have to consider is a lot of this will happen incrementally as I mentioned earlier. For example, some of the pioneers who start living to 110 years will need to plan for an additional 20 years of finances, if they had only planned for it till 90 years of age, then as they keep living longer, they will find ways to finance themselves further.

We also have to take into account another fundamental point. Given that we are planning to live longer in a "healthy" body and "mind" we will also be working longer. And that is an important point to think about. Even now in my experience there is at least a 10-year difference in retirement ages across the World. In places like India the retirement age is 60. I have seen my perfectly fit father retire at 60 when he could have easily been working productively till 65 or 70. In the US and UK people generally retire at around 65 to 66 and I have seen people continue to work till they are 70 as well. This difference in retirement age already exists.

As we increase longevity with good health people will begin to work longer and it will be perfectly ok to hire a 60-year-old with the expectation that they have a 15-to-20-year career still ahead of them.

I can already hear people thinking in their minds about how it's difficult, even to get a job after 50 or 55 these days. I agree that is a challenge. At the same time as I keep saying this increase in longevity will take some time to get used to, and apart from us who embrace some of these changes, society too will have to embrace them.

The only thing I am sure about is that a section of society will embrace these changes and new opportunities for people over 60, 70 and 80 years of age will emerge and they will be able to enjoy a happy working life if that is what they want.

Coming back to the original question of how we will finance our longevity.

It will happen through us working longer. It will happen as the insurance companies and actuaries around the World wake up to the fact that there will be a group of people who will live much longer than they do today. They will start designing products for them to buy into, that will fund their later years. Society as a whole will be open to employing people who are older in age, though not necessarily older in health. As a group and as a society we will need to start thinking differently as well.

What would I invest in today if I wanted something that would give me large benefits 50 years from now? Land comes to mind as an obvious choice. There are many land parcels in this World that one could afford today, but would not buy given they would probably not appreciate in value for the next 15 to 20 years. But if we know that we are thinking in terms of a 50-year timeline that investment would look very different. Perhaps things like the Metaverse and Cryptocurrency would be places to invest in, especially in the long run. Climate Change and Net Zero are huge topics today and investing in them for the long term would make a lot of sense.

The bottom line again is, we will find a way to finance our longer life once we accept the fact we will live longer. Once we know our timelines we will begin to plan accordingly and things will fall in place. There will be many challenges. There always will be. But we will find solutions to them. And some of us will prevail and pave the way for upcoming generations.

The last major question I am going try and answer with regard to this topic, was actually posed by my wife.

How will we find purpose in our lives when we realize we are now going to live for 200 years?

It's probably one of the most relevant questions and as I reflected on it, I realized, probably one of the most difficult ones we will face when given the choice of longevity. For a lot of us we may have entered our 50's or 60's or 70s. Our children are about to get settled and we are looking forward to a retired life to be spent with friends our age, visits to our children and grandchildren, with hopefully only the occasional visit to the doctor. Some of us may like cruising or traveling the World and we would do that. Some of us may have hobbies like carpentry, building houses, painting, wine making, cooking etc. and we would indulge in them for the years that we think we have ahead.

But then suddenly we are now faced with the prospect of living healthily for another 50 to 80 or 100 years. What are we going to do? What will be our purpose in life? What will we do that will make us want to keep going?

It's a difficult one. I have personally not yet found what my true purpose in life is. So, if I suddenly realized I would now live for another 80 or100 years in good health, it would set me thinking. Whilst finances would be a key factor, and it would probably take up a significant part of my thoughts, I would try and think beyond that for a bit.

Let's assume I am 55. My children are on their way to getting established in their lives. I have also found a way to make sure I will have enough money and investments to live comfortably for the next 80 years in good health. I am also well connected and am confident I can start a new business or venture that will interest me and keep me interested for about 10 to 20 years, after which I would probably look for something new. I would then go ahead and start up again and maybe this time stay with it for 30 years.

In the meantime, I would be able to spend enough time with the people I love, my children and grandchildren, with the friends I have and also keep making new friends. I would have time to travel the World and see new places, experience new adventures, new technologies and the like. I would also probably make a trip to space by then.

But then what would be the purpose of my life?

Would I just be living longer for the sake of living longer? Would I reach a stage where nothing would really give me joy? Would I reach a stage where I would have probably seen most of the things there are to see? Experienced most of the human emotions I would want to experience? Would I reach a stage after 60 years where I would say, I don't want to live anymore?

I don't know the answer to that question. The thing is I will only know that answer for myself when I reach there.

If and when I do reach there, I do promise, I will come back and answer this question. I also think that different people will have different answers to that question, and everyone's answers will be based on their own unique experiences, beliefs and thoughts. None of the answers will be right or wrong. They will just be answers that our generation who go through this for the first time will have to answer.

For future generations who are born into this World knowing that they will live up to 150 or 200 years right from the start will have a different outlook. For them that will be their reality and they will find their purpose in life the way we do today.

But coming back to the question of how we will find purpose in a longer life, it is something that each one of us who take up this journey will need to think about.

I will now stop talking about longevity and come back to the original question we had started out with.

Can we really become successful? Can we find that "something more" that we are looking for? Can we, do it?

I think we can. And I think it starts with us examining our beliefs.

The reason I spent so much time on longevity is because a topic like that seriously challenges our belief system. But so does anything else we try to do differently. And doing things a little differently is what is going to make us successful. Doing things slightly differently will help us get to that "something more" that we are looking for.

So yes, we can! And that's what we will explore going ahead. Buckle up for the ride!

***

The question is "How?"

"We are looking for a way to success, a success that is defined by us, within a finite amount of time, without disrupting our status quo of a lifestyle."

How do we do it is the Million Dollar question. Will reading this book tell you how? It won't.

I can almost hear you thinking. "So why the @#$5^&*(@ have you been stringing us along?" "Are you kidding me?"

My answer to that is as follows. Just reading this book won't help you to be successful. It won't help you to get where you want to be or get you that "something more" you crave for. *Acting on what this book talks about, diligently practicing what this book talks about, staying with what this book talks about and then coming back to it again and again, when it seems like you are failing, might just get you somewhere near to success.* So yes, this book will give you one of the many possible paths to the success you are looking for. But only about 2 to 3% of the 20% who are still reading will probably get there. The rest of you will probably read it, feel good or bad about it for a bit and then relegate it to a bookshelf or a file on your Kindle or whatever equivalent you are using for reading this. There is not much this book can do for you, lying on a bookshelf!

Sorry to be blunt. But I did warn you I had lost it. And I am not in the business of trying to please you. I am trying to show you a possible path. A path that I think might work.

So, if you are still interested, let's go ahead on the journey.

The first thing we need to do is try and find out what we really want. Yes, what is it that we *really* want. Is it money, is it fame, is it love, is it the ability to do what you feel like when you feel like, is it the ability to just keep painting all day, is it the time to keep exploring the World, is it the ability to keep writing all day, is it the ability to keep trading stocks all day, is it real estate, is it finance, is it architecture, is it designing, is it nursing, is it singing, is it dancing, is it philanthropy. What is it? Is it more than one thing?

Think about it. Force yourself to focus. Give yourself a couple of days or maybe even a week and then write it down. Write down what you think you really want. It may look like something below.

I want to be able to travel the World at my pace, in the most luxurious manner, and not have to worry about money any more. I want to be in perfect health and I want my near and dear ones to be happy. I also want to be famous and well known and want people to like me. I then want to be able to talk about my travels and if possible, hold some talks where I have something to offer to people and slowly build up a name for myself, where people come to me whenever they think travel.

Or

I love interior designing and I want to be able to design fabulous interiors and then execute them. I want to do this all day without having to worry about money. I want to have a high end and very exclusive client base and have enough time to focus on every project that I take up. I want to be well known and appreciated in my own circle. I want to have a wonderful life with my partner as well.

Or

I want to be a well-known activist, known for what I am passionate about. I really want to help people and devote myself to public life. At the same time, I want to leave behind a legacy. A legacy that people will remember me for. I also want to do this without having to bother about money or by accepting money from anyone who would want me to compromise my values.

Or

I really just want to be a rap singer and a World Famous one at that. That's it. That's all I want.

Or

I had wanted to be a great player of (whatever sport you loved!). I now want to be associated with that sport either as a commentator or as a manager, or as someone who has some say about the sport and do things that allow me to experience the sport as much as I can.

Or

I want to be a famous Religious/Lifestyle speaker who people love and come to for advice.

Or

I want to be hugely successful at trading and real estate and amass a huge amount of wealth so that I don't have to work another day in my life. I then want to spend time drinking the best of wines and spending time on my expensive yacht.

Or

I just want a very peaceful life with no stress, with a lot of time at my disposal to spend time with my spouse, my children and even my Grandchildren. I want to have a small Garden where I can sit peacefully and also have a few friends with whom I can spend some quality time ruminating in silence.

Or

I assume you have got the drift!

It's crucial you take a shot at writing this down for yourself. Some of you may already have this written down. If you have then you are well on your way to reaching your goal. Some of you may not and as you start to do this, some of you may find it easy, some of you may not.

If you don't find it easy, trust me, you are not alone. It is a difficult task. For some of us we may have often thought about things that we might want to do, but we have never really even articulated it to ourselves, even in our own thoughts. We have never really allowed ourselves to tell ourselves, what is it we really want, what is it that we crave for.

So, for some of us this can be really difficult. I understand.

The key is to get stuck into this. Take your time, at the same time don't avoid it. Think about it, sleep over it. Talk to someone about it if you can, but don't give up. Even if the first thing you think about may not be the exact thing you want, don't worry. Just start writing it down and see what happens. Keep coming back to what you are writing and keep re-writing. As you force yourself to do it and think about it, something will start forming in your mind and you will be able articulate in some fashion what is it that you really want. What is it that will give you that something more you want out of life.

Sometimes talking to yourself in the mirror might help as well. It may sound funny, but it's not. It's like trying articulate what's there in your mind to yourself. It takes a bit of practice but it could work for some of you. For some of you thinking about it whilst you walk, run or exercise may help as well. Sometimes cooking or cleaning out the closet also helps with your thinking. It will be different for different people. The key is to do it.

Two important things here.

One: Initially don't constrain yourself based on what you know about yourself or your situation. At least not initially. I know it will have a bearing on what you ultimately do, but don't let that constrain you at the outset. As an example. Maybe you want to go to Egypt and spend a lot of time exploring and researching the pyramids. Maybe that's what you really want. But you hesitate to write that down, because of reasons like, you don't have the money to travel, or you don't know anything about archeology, or that you may not be able to handle the heat. I agree those may be challenges to what you want, but don't let that stand in your way, when you are initially thinking about this. Give your imagination a bit of a free run. Sounds a little impractical, but it's necessary. Force yourself to do it. Don't get hung up on the phrase, "but that's not practical." It's a good phrase, but it's also a dampener when you are on this particular journey.

Two: If any of you are thinking about anything that is remotely illegal, criminal, or in any way involves hurting or taking advantage of any other human being then that is unacceptable and is not part of this book. If you have any such desires, I suggest you stop reading the book and we can part ways.

Coming back to your efforts in terms of writing things down. Force yourself to think about this. Some of you may take a day, some of you may take two days, but do force yourself to do this part within a week. Write it down and then we can go to the next step. Again, some of you may get stuck at this step. Understandable. Read on and then come back to this later.

Once you have something written down, the next step is to analyze it.

Let's assume you have something like this written down. I have kept it generic and you can fill in the blanks with whatever is it you desire. Again, this is just one possible way to approach this. The important thing though is to have something written down. Something you can keep coming back to.

I want to be able to (insert whatever it is you want) at my pace, in the most wonderful manner, possible and not have to worry about money any more. I want to be in perfect health. I want to be famous and well known and want people to like me. I then want to be able to talk about my *(insert whatever it is you want)* *and if possible, hold some talks where I have something to offer to people and slowly build up a name for myself, where people come to me whenever they think* *(insert whatever it is you want)*

Let's assume you have something like this written down for yourself. I keep saying it's important to take a shot at writing it down and then reading it. It will allow you to figure out if it is really what you want. And I will give an example of that.

I always thought I like travel as one of my desires. But then when I started traveling like crazy all over the World, doing overnight flights, fighting jet lag etc. I began to wonder if it really was traveling that I liked? As I analyzed it a little deeper, I realized I did like traveling. What I didn't like were some of the inconveniences associated with it. I realized if I could travel a little better and with more time, it would not bother me. I started doing that and realized I did indeed like travel. I did like the fact of coming home to my corner, but I also liked the thrill of seeing new places, meeting new people etc.

The next question I asked myself was could I do this all my life. And that is a tougher question. I tried to imagine traveling for about 6 months in a year. Granted I would travel Business Class, stay at the best of hotels, etc. But would I still like it. I gave it a lot of thought and realized I could probably do it for about 3 to 4 months in a year, but not 6 months. It also needed to be at my pace. I could then do other things like blog about my travels, take photographs, talk about it etc. So yes, I could do that for a living. How it would make me money, I had no idea. But that comes later. The first thing I established was that I *did* like to travel, and that I could do it for a considerable amount of time in the near future. I could end up changing my mind after a few years but right now that was what I wanted.

This is the stage we need to get to with whatever it is that we think we like. It could be anything from research on a particular topic, to sports, to real estate investing, to cooking, to shopping, to dancing, to being a social media influencer or anything else you might like doing.

So now that you have the sentence written out above, or even if you have it in your mind, let's see how we can make it a little simpler. Whilst I like the detail and feelings that the above sentence outlines, the reason I want to make it a little simpler, is for us to be able to keep repeating it to ourselves over and over again. And the simpler it is, the easier that will be.

Let's see how we can do that.

I want to be able to (insert whatever it is you want) at my pace, in the most wonderful manner, possible and not have to worry about money any more. I want to be in perfect health. I want to be famous and well known and want people to like me. I then want to be able to talk about my (insert whatever it is you want) and if possible, hold some talks where I have something to offer to people and slowly build up a name for myself, where people come to me whenever they think (insert whatever it is you want)

What I have done above is highlight the parts I think we can take out in order to simplify what we have written. Once we do that this is what it will look like. A little simpler, but the essence of what we want is still there.

I want to (insert whatever it is you want), in the most wonderful manner, possible. I want to be in perfect health. I want to be famous and well known. I want to be able to talk about my (insert whatever it is you want) and hold talks where I have something to offer and build a name for myself.

Again, this is one approach. Feel free to try out any others. At the same time, simplifying this helps focus our thoughts. If you look at the above now, you will see there is still some opportunity to make it a little more crisp and shorter. You will also notice the above is much more definitive as compared to the first version. So, let's try one more iteration. I will leave you to figure out what exactly I have done, but the below is what I think is a slightly better version.

I want to (insert whatever it is you want), in the most wonderful manner. I want to be in perfect health. I want to be able to talk about my (insert whatever it is you want) and share it with the World. I want to be famous and well known.

Once we have the above, we will make one more change and then we will have our sentence ready. If you notice, the sentence above talks about how we want to be able to do what we want. Here we will indulge ourselves for a bit and restructure the sentence by replacing "want to/ want to be" with "am." I know it's a bit presumptive, but just indulge me for now.

I am** (insert whatever it is you want), **in the most wonderful manner. I am in perfect health. I am able to talk about my** (insert whatever it is you want) **and share it with the World. I am famous and well known.

Now we have that sentence. It encapsulates what is it we think we want. What we think will give us that something more in life which we have been looking for. Something that will perhaps lead to us to being successful in the way we want.

It's important to read the above sentence with the "I am," even though it is yet to happen. The reason for that is the "law of attraction." For those of you who have read about the "law of attraction" you are probably familiar with this. For those of you who haven't, it is a concept that really says, *we get whatever we think about.* It essentially hinges on the fact that we shape our reality with our thinking. Whatever we give our thought to has a way of coming true.

Whether we believe in it or not, there is a level of truth in the fact, that for us to get anything at all we have to first think about it. It's a bit like, we wouldn't get that new book if we didn't think about it or go out and buy it. It's more or less true for most of the things that we do in life. We first think about it and then we find a way to do it. Sometimes it may even come to us as a gift from someone.

The "law of attraction" states that we get whatever we are thinking about, and hence the way to think about this sentence is to think about it as if it's already happening to us. Hence the "I am." We need to imagine we are already there, and then analyze the "feelings" we have when we think we have already reached our goal. If we can hold on to those "imagined feelings" we would have, once we reach our goals, it's a good start.

So have a look at your final sentence once again. Commit it to memory and then keep saying it over and over to yourself for a few days. Don't worry about whether it sounds silly or if nothing is happening. Just do it. Just keep saying it to yourself. Make it a habit. Take the plunge and keep saying it over and over to yourself whenever you can.

It's important for the idea to get embedded in your mind.

Once you are comfortable with the idea we will proceed to the next step. But before that I will give you an opportunity to not only get used to the sentence and the idea, but also to make tweaks. You may want to modify it. You will realize as you keep saying it that you may want to modify it slightly or add in an important or relevant detail. For example, if you are thinking about becoming an influencer, you may want to get a little more specific about what media? Or you may want to broaden the scope. If you were interested in setting up a new type of bitcoin, you could start thinking about a name for it. Essentially, it's about mulling over what you think you want, now that you have a more or less specific sentence. Remember, what you have thought about is always subject to change as you start on your journey to that "something more."

We now have a certain idea about what we want. The next step is to get down to the actual work of achieving that idea. And that takes me to the next step or chapter where we talk about how we will need to make some changes to ourselves, to our beliefs. Changing ourselves is one of the biggest challenges we all face. We know intuitively we need to do that, but we don't. We hear about fancy sentences that "Change is the only constant," but when it comes to meaningfully making changes in our own lives, we tend to procrastinate. I know it since I do it myself. I know you do it; else you wouldn't be reading this book!

So, let's try and explore the subject of change before we head out into the specifics of how we achieve our dreams!

***

Changing yourself is not easy

Why is it so difficult to make changes to our own life?

Have you ever worn something you like, especially at home that is clearly at the end of its life, but you still keep wearing it, because it's comfortable, it's familiar, it feels worn in, it feels right. If you have, you are with me.

Till recently I was wearing a pair of slacks to bed and it had become my favorite. It was the right feel. It was soft, it was snug, it fitted well, it looked good despite being worn, and I just liked it, period! The only reason I stopped wearing it was because I left it in a hotel by mistake!!

I now wear something else to bed. It was forced change. It does happen at some point, to all of us and we adapt. So, we know we can do it. The important thing though is how do we make meaningful changes to our life in order to achieve that "something more" we are aspiring for.

There are two types of changes we will need to master. Both will need "will power," but the first one is somewhat easier compared to the second one. So, let's start with the first type of change. I will use myself as an example here, only because I tried it and it worked. It's an example of how I made a few changes to my lifestyle to achieve a certain goal. It has not helped me move to my final goal of "something more," but I think in some way or other, it might be a stepping stone to that.

As I said before this type of changing yourself is somewhat short term and we have all probably done something like this before. But I still want to share the example since it did throw up some pointers to me, in terms of how to stick with something, despite the constant tendency to give up.

Over the last many years, I had put on weight. I was a 192.6 pounds to be exact. At 6 feet one, it wasn't that apparent, but for me, I had a problem. All my jeans had become tight and my belly seemed to bulge out when I sat down! This had not happened to me before. I guess with age, with my love of wine, beer, chocolates etc. I was beginning to see the results on my body. This was coupled with some level of stress at work, the fact my metabolism wasn't what it used to be etc. etc.

So, I realized I needed to make some changes. Initially I made a few changes. I fasted for a day or so once a week. Tried not to have a drink every other night. Increased my walking and workouts. But then I would have a late dinner for a couple of days, have a few drinks, and soon I was back to square one! If this sounds familiar then we are on the right track. Let's see what happened next.

I realized in order to really lose some serious weight, I needed to make some significant changes to what I was doing. I decided I would do four things as below:

1. Take a one hour walk in the morning, without fail.

2. Stop having dinner. (WARNING: Do not do this without consulting your doctor!)

3. Stop Drinking as much as possible

4. Add in a workout where possible

There were two other things I did; one was I kept track of the above in an excel sheet. This helped me see where I was going. I tracked it by filling in columns with Walk, No Dinner, No Drink. I also did this diligently. When I missed doing what I had set out on, I added that in in red and bold, like **DRINK!** This helped me keep track of when I was failing.

The other thing I did, and which was something that helped me enormously was I took my weight every morning right after my walk. Each time I did this and I saw an improvement, I felt good! It encouraged me to keep up my routine. When my stomach started growling with hunger at night, I would remember what my weight had been the previous day, and I would push myself to go hungry, knowing I would better my weight by about 0.2 pounds the next day, if I could just keep it up! Mind you, it's not easy. It used up a lot of my will power. And I did give up on some days, but then I picked it up again after a day or two.

Slowly I could see my jeans beginning to feel a little normal again. Slowly I began to be able to fall asleep on a hungry stomach. I could begin to feel the fat burn away when I walked for an hour in the morning, especially after going hungry for about 16 hours! I used sheer will power. I just forced myself to do it.

Did it work?

It did. After three months of doing this, I reached the weight below:

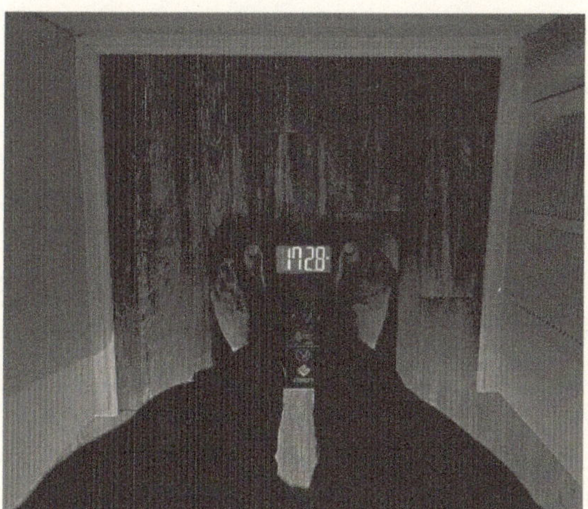

That was almost 20 pounds!!

Make no mistake, I have put back about 5 to 6 pounds now, but I am in much better shape. The thing is I had to make changes to myself, to my habits. I had to force myself to do the four things above. I had to grit my teeth to do each one of them and stick to it. But I did it.

So, I know from experience we can make changes. A lot of you have also probably done something like this in some shape or form. It's not a big deal, but it is something we all need to be able to do, in order to make meaningful changes to ourselves.

So, this was the first type of change I was talking about. As you will recall I also said that this type of change was relatively easier compared to the second type of change that I will now talk about. There is a reason for that.

If you look closely at the four things I did, and I will write them out below once more to jog your memory, you will notice a pattern in them.

1. Take a one hour walk in the morning, without fail. (Needs "will power" but is a physical thing.)

2. Stop having dinner. (WARNING: Do not do this without consulting your doctor!) (Needs "will power" but is a physical thing.)

3. Stop Drinking as much as possible (Needs "will power" but is a physical thing.)

4. Add in a workout where possible (Needs "will power" but is a physical thing.)

When I say "needs will power, but is a physical thing" what I mean is that it is an action we can take, without having to really do a lot of *mental* gymnastics. Yes, we will have to fight against the hunger, or the laziness, but that's about it. It requires a lot of mental focus, don't get me wrong, but it's not like using the mind to do complicated math's, or forcing the mind to write something, or compose something. For some reason, I think it's easier to do something like this, than force myself to write.

I could be wrong about this and maybe for some of you it is easier to force the mind to discipline itself and make oneself write, or compose or engage in scientific enquiry. It may indeed be the case and if you are in that category, you are a step ahead of us, and definitely a step ahead of me.

This brings me to the second type of change.

The second type of change is a mental change. It requires us to change how we think and then how we act. It also requires us to take decisions.

For me this type of change is harder. It's a bit like me, who is an introvert, trying to be an extrovert. It can be done; it just makes my mind work harder. If, however I want to be doing something which requires me to be an extrovert, then I will have to change my mindset and make some changes in myself.

Let me use another example.

I like writing. I like the recognition that comes with being an author. I like the creative aspect of being a writer. But there is a lot more to being a writer.

You have to find time to write. You have to keep writing when you don't want to. This is important. *You have to keep writing even when you don't want to.* This is important. In almost any profession, be it painting, politics, science, engineering, showbiz, etc. there comes a time when you have had enough of doing the same thing. And yet you have to go on. That is where, for a lot of us, the mind takes the easy way out.

Try as hard as I might, I get stuck when I am writing, and then I stop writing.... sometimes for days! And that is what I have come to realize, is unacceptable. There has to be a way for me to keep going. Something has to change within me to keep me going. And that is the hard part that I am talking about.

I have read various pieces about this. All the big writers are pretty much unanimous about writing. The all say, keep writing whether you like it or not. Come back and edit it, but keep going. Keep aside a fixed time every day, but don't stop. You have to keep going.

Easier said than done. I have tried it for many years and have kept failing. And that made me realize two things.

The first, that changing how we think is perhaps one of the most important things we need to do whilst on our journey to that "something more" we want.

The second thing, was the realization of how difficult it was to do this.

It's difficult because it requires a high level of will power. It requires more will power according to me to make the mind think and do things differently, than physically forcing yourself to exercise or walk. At least that's how it works for me.

When you sit down and force yourself to write, you are essentially forcing your mind to be creative. It's fun to be creative. We all love it. But what we are talking about here is to force oneself to be creative for at least 50 to 80 thousand words if not more. That is about 150 to 200 pages. That is not easy. However, much you like writing and being creative, when you have to keep going for those lengths, you realize you need a greater level of mental discipline than what we are used to.

To complicate matters, it's also not just about slogging along. Whatever you are doing, be it writing or anything else, it needs to be quality stuff. At the end of the day, that's what you are aiming for. It needs to be something people will want to read, if you are a writer. It needs to be a painting people will want to buy if you are a painter, or a song people will want to listen to if you are a singer, or an invention that will make money for you or change the World if you are an inventor/ scientist. If you are a trader you need to be able to make money, if you are a politician you need to be able to make people want to vote for you, if you are an athlete/sportsperson you want to compete and win, if you are a mountain climber, you want to climb a significant peak. If you are a chef you want to make dishes people want to eat.

So not only is it about forcing yourself to keep at what you want, you need to be able to produce quality stuff that sets you apart from others. And that requires a greater level of mental discipline than what we are used to. If you already have that level and are doing so, then I doubt you need this book.

At the same time, it's important to realize *you probably do have it within you*, to do all the above. For example, I am fairly confident that given time I am able to churn out some decent writing. (Don't go by what you are reading here!). I am also confident that at some point I will get around to finishing what I need to do. The challenge I face is, I tend to give up half way. Or quarter way, and sometimes even three-fourth of the way!

For some of you this may sound familiar.

Some of you may have got over this part and have actually done something. The challenge you are facing is about the next phase. How do you market what you have done? How do you ensure you are wildly successful? And in case you are not, how do you move onto your second project and then your third, and so on!

The point is, doing all of the above requires us to change how we think, how we act, and how we live our life.

This is the second change that I was talking about. This is the change I was saying is hard. This is the change we will need to make in ourselves in order to reach that "something more."

This brings me back to the topic of this chapter which was, **"Changing yourself is not easy."** Admittedly, and at least for me it is not. At the same time being able to do this is probably the most crucial thing each one of us will need to do.

As we go forward in this book, I am going to try and outline five possible paths to help us on our journey to that "something more." Some of the paths have been tried by me with limited success, some are a work in progress. But what I have realized is these seem to be the paths. I have a feeling that a combination of these paths, along with whatever tweaks to these paths each one of you will inject into them whilst practicing them, will lead you to a better place, with regard to achieving that "something more" you want out of life.

So, let's give it a try.

Path 1

Find Appreciation/Recognition for what you like

I have said it before. We all crave appreciation and recognition. Whether we want to admit it to ourselves or not, we need someone to appreciate us. When someone appreciates us, we feel good, we feel safe and it allows us to do our best work.

Unfortunately, we don't get enough appreciation. People talk about it, but the bottom line is we don't get enough appreciation in today's World, despite all the various communication tools at our beck and call. We live in nuclear families, we have fewer friends, everyone is busy, the children are busy, spouses are stressed, so who is appreciating you? A simple "Good Job" at work may seem like appreciation, but it is not. It just seems like that to our starved psyche, which has taken it for granted we won't get the appreciation we deserve.

We have become so hardened to not receiving appreciation that even when someone does, we become awkward. Have you heard someone say "it's my job," when you appreciate them? That's what I mean. It's nice and modest, but it's also a defense mechanism for us to counter genuine appreciation.

The other challenge is we have not trained ourselves enough to appreciate others around us, to appreciate the gifts we already have, or even the ability to appreciate ourselves. The tendency in today's World, for some reason, is to generally focus on the negative side of things. There is a reason for that.

One of the major reasons we think negatively, is due to our consumption of media. Nothing sells like bad news or sensational news. With smart algorithms which track which article you might have read, you will find that if you read one negative piece of news, they will push you other similar pieces, which leads us into a vicious cycle of consuming negative news.

The other big thing that has happened Globally, because of media, is a great sense of skepticism we have all developed. Given the Global scandals, Wars and even the behaviors of some prominent World Leaders, it is almost impossible to figure out what is the real truth anymore. What this does, is lead to further negativity, and it takes away from the simple act of us giving and receiving appreciation.

Finally, the Corporate World does not help either. In the name of accountability, the Corporate World keeps people under a constant sense of pressure to perform, and however good you are, there is always another level that needs to cleared. What this really does, is make us look for people to blame, rather than look for people to praise. There are obviously exceptions to this, but what I am talking about are trends.

Have you heard of the saying in the Corporate World, "you are only as good as your last quarter?" If you have you will know what I mean.

The thing we need to understand here, and it's important, is that receiving appreciation for what we do is of significant importance. Why? Because it simply spurs us on to do more of the same thing.

Many years ago, I had written a play. It was a good concept, or at least I had thought so, but it was raw, unfinished and amateur. What my wife suggested at that time, and she was always a great supporter of my wild ideas, was we get a professional opinion from a TV series Director whom she happened to know through her professional contacts. We did that.

I will not name him. But what he did when he heard the script was essentially start saying some nice things about it. For some reason he liked the Villain in the story, which was a character named "Grohorrvirus" and all I remember from that interaction is that he was so appreciative of what I was trying to do. Given his stature, those words of appreciation stayed with me and my wife, and it inspired us to go on and stage three amateur theatre productions, the final one of which was somewhat bearable! The point though I am trying to make here, is that without those initial words of appreciation or encouragement, I don't think I would have gone very far with those productions.

And that is why one of the first things we need to do is go out and find appreciation and recognition for what we want to do. Even if it means starting with yourself. It may sound a little silly, but we often short change ourselves, even more than others.

If you are still reading, I am sure you are one of those people who have already achieved a significant level of success in what you do. You know you have the capability to do more. You know you have other significant talents, likes or desires. The question is, have you recently taken time out to appreciate yourself? And I mean really appreciate yourself and what you have achieved and more importantly on what you can achieve? The answer is probably a no.

So, it might make sense for you to take a moment and just think about how much you can appreciate yourself for what you have already achieved. For some of us, this may seem a little narcissistic and self-involved. But we are talking about the self here. We are talking about ourselves and our ability to be more than we currently are.

So, give yourself a break and try and look at yourself through the lens of what you have already achieved. Perhaps you have a great job, a wonderful family. Perhaps you have already brought your first home, or even your second one, or more. Perhaps people know about your blog and you already have a sizable following. Perhaps you are a well-known personality in your neighborhood. Maybe you have a lot of friends on Facebook and other social media handles and you are able to regularly post about things. Perhaps you are raising children and making sure they are raised the right way. Perhaps you are taking care of someone. Maybe you are fighting for climate change. Maybe you are advocating for diversity or are involved in charity. Maybe you take Yoga classes. Maybe you collect certain items. Whatever it is that you may be doing, you deserve boundless appreciation and recognition for that. I am sure others are doing that in some shape or form, but you also need to take some time out and appreciate yourself for any of the things that you are doing.

Again, you may be thinking about how this will help you.

It will help you by reinforcing to yourself that you can do what is needed to go that extra mile. It will let you evaluate your own capabilities, your own potential, your own ability to make significant and meaningful changes to yourself in order to get to that "something more."

Often when you read about a lot of very successful people, you will see one common trait they had, which was the ability to stick with what they were doing. You will also realize you have probably been doing the same. You have stayed with a reasonable job or Business or venture for a number of years, you have been steady, you have taken the good with the bad, and you have stuck it out. And whilst you have been successful, you are yet to reach that level of success you crave. But the take away here is that you too have the ability to be tenacious. And you need to appreciate and recognize that about yourself. Unless you do that yourself, even other people will find it difficult to recognize that.

The point is you need to appreciate and recognize yourself. Put aside one evening in your life where you sit down and celebrate yourself. It may seem a little weird, but I suggest you take out one evening in your life, either alone, or with a loved one, or with a friend, where you sit down and have a celebratory dinner to all the successes you have had till now.

Raise a toast to all the hardships and challenges you have managed to overcome to reach to where you are. It could not have been easy and yet you persevered and here you are. The very fact that you are in a place where you are is an achievement, and that happened because you were very good at what you have been doing till now. Take time out to genuinely appreciate all the efforts you have made along the way. The late hours you have spent, the sacrifices you have made, the hardships you have endured, just to get to where you are. It has not been easy, and yet you have reached to where you are.

Take a breather and appreciate what you have done.

I am going to stop here for a second and digress a little. By now you know I like doing that.

The thing about this exercise, is that you really have to do it in order to get anywhere. What I mean is it's experiential. What I mean is you really have to put this book down now, and actually go and do what I am suggesting. It may be daytime, so then you need to stop reading this book, and look for the most suitable time that you go and have this dinner. I really mean it. Once you have done that, you can start reading where you left off.

I know it's not the best thing to suggest to someone in the middle of reading something, but unfortunately, that is how this works. Unless you go out and try this thing, you really won't get the true flavor of the next exercise. So why don't you indulge me and put the book down now and go and plan your own celebratory dinner, where you just sit down and appreciate yourself. Where you recognize all the great things you have done till now.

Think about how you finished school or graduated and got your first job. Or how you snagged your first assignment. Think about how you made your first painting, or how took your first photograph. Think about how you scrimped on all your savings and bought your first house or car or motorcycle. How you put your child in the best possible school. How you turned around your struggling business. How you made your first sale. How you wrote your first story. How you passed your exams with flying colors. How you won that game. How you were recognized for all the volunteering work you had done. Remember and rejoice in the memories of all the wonderful things that you have *already* done and achieved.

If you do this exercise seriously and possibly with someone close to you reinforcing all the above, it can be quite intense. Remember, we are not used to appreciation. We are not used to congratulating ourselves properly. Therefor when we do this properly, we will get a sense of how much we have already achieved. We will realize how successful we already are.

The most important thing though that we need to realize after this exercise is as below. And if for some reason you don't realize it, or feel that way, then you need to either go back and do the exercise again, or ideally stop reading and throw this book away.

You will realize that the thing within you, that brought you to where you are, will take you to where you want to be, which is be wildly successful!

Yes, you already have what it takes to be wildly successful. What you need to do is harness those qualities within you and give it a last shot along with me. Yes, this is kind of our last shot. If we don't do it now, it's going to be a long time before we try it again.

The next chapter is going to be about how we take the plunge, but before you do that, there are two things you will need to do. One, you will need to find people who appreciate what you are going to do. You need to find someone who will encourage you on with your idea. Two, you need to refer back to the sentence you created when you were reading chapter 4, "The Question is "How?" (I have reproduced the sentence below for easy reference. If you didn't do that exercise then, do it now!)

I am *(insert whatever it is you want),* ***in the most wonderful manner. I am in perfect health. I am able to talk about my*** *(insert whatever it is you want)* ***and share it with the World. I am famous and well known.***

With regard to finding someone who will appreciate you, I mean someone who will encourage you. It could be someone in your family, a friend or even someone you know at work. If you are one of those people who don't want to share what you want to try out with anyone, I get that as well. In that case you will need to appreciate your self, or reach out to groups who do the same thing that you are wanting or trying to do, over the internet, where there is a level of anonymity. Whatever you do, find a way to encourage yourself to try out what you are planning to do in the sentence you have written out above.

Even if you have not written anything out, I am sure you know deep down, what is it that you would like to do. Start doing it. And if no one else appreciates you, appreciate yourself. ☺

Path 2

Plunge In

It's very difficult to learn swimming if you are not willing, at some point to, to take a plunge into water. It's the same with whatever it is you want to do, that you think will make you wildly successful.

Let's take an example here. If you are thinking about Real Estate investing, then you need to start doing it. It is no doubt a difficult field, but you have to start. You may be an absolute beginner, you may be someone who has bought one house, or you may be someone who has bought a few houses, but wants to make it big. Where ever you are in this journey you will need to take some hard decisions and start off. You notice I said the words "hard decisions."

I say it because, taking decisions is one of the hardest things humans face. I did not realize this for a long time. Sometime in my mid to late thirties, one of my senior colleagues made this statement, that we, as in "people" don't like to make decisions. It was a corporate real estate decision we were going to make about appointing a particular supplier. But when he said this, it got me thinking. Years later I did some research and realized how true it was. We are all hesitant to take decisions. I have outlined below some of the reasons why we are like this.

Whenever we take a decision, we are owning the consequences of that decision. Even a choice of what we eat or drink, which is a relatively easy decision, has a consequence on our wellbeing. As we are going through life today, we are faced with multiple decisions throughout our day. We face the simplest of decisions around food or clothes, taking a call or not, to taking some hard work-related decisions, that could be quite important. We are often on conference calls during the day, where we are forced to be taking decisions on what we need to do regarding work. Then there are other decisions, with regards to our homes, our investments, our children, our parents, our friends, our entertainment, etc.

As a result, today we live in an environment where we are constantly taking decisions, on something or the other, which leads us into a situation of a "decision overload." What it means, is something like this.

There are so many micro decisions we are taking during the day, every day, starting from what is it that we want to google, to which route we need to take to work, etc. *that we are unable to focus on some of the really big decisions we need to take.* I will share an example below.

I know I need to invest in real estate, if I want to grow my real estate portfolio. I keep looking at real estate options during the weekend, but then during the week, I get busy with all the other decisions, I need to make with regard to my day job, my family etc. and I postpone my real estate decision to the weekend. By then I am tired and I am trying to take a big real estate decision, which is in reality a complex one. I spend two weekends looking at real estate and realize that I don't find anything that suits my needs, and then I start procrastinating on the same. I think I will come back to it over the next weekend. But then the next weekend is a holiday and we end up traveling, which in itself has involved a number of decisions and therefore I defer the real estate decision by another week. By the time I get around to making a decision, the option that I somewhat liked, has gone. The process starts again, and I am yet to make a decision.

It's the same with a lot of other things we intend to do.

I have often thought of joining a gym and getting a trainer to help me get into shape. I have been thinking about it for years. I have not yet done it.

I keep thinking about one day, when I will go to Egypt and see the pyramids. It's one thing I really want to do. I have not done it yet.

I keep thinking about that You Tube channel I think I should create. I know I can make it, I know I can make it interesting, but there are a few things I need to do before I do that, like getting a good camera, and a mike. I have still not done it.

I think I should get down to writing that thriller I have in mind. I even wrote the outline. But I have not got around to doing it.

Does any of this sound familiar to you? It may be something else totally, that you have been thinking about, but you get the gist, right? Why do you think this happens?

It's because we don't like to take the really important hard decisions. It's because we don't want to plunge in. It's because we find it more and more difficult to get out of our comfort zone. Our comfort zone creeps up on us as we move into our thirties, forties, fifties and beyond. We are comfortable the way we are. We comfortable with the pace we are at. We do want something, but we don't want to do anything drastic.

And that's when we start to procrastinate our decision making.

I do it a lot myself. I see a great real estate opportunity staring me in the face. But to make it happen I need to take some hard decisions around travel, lawyers, brokers etc. and I find myself putting it off. I get a great idea that I need to write about, but then I keep waiting for that perfect moment, when I will feel fresh and be able to sit in front of my computer and write it. And the moment goes by.

That's the problem we all face. It's not easy to take the plunge.

Then there is the bigger issue for us, is that we have taken the plunge a few times, and things have not worked out! So now, we are even more discouraged about taking the next one. Sounds familiar? We started that You tube channel, but then after a few, it just petered out. We started painting that beautiful thought we had, but then stopped midway, and it's still lying there. We had that great idea about something. We even wrote down a business plan. People actually liked it. But then we got so caught up in work we have not had time to focus on it.

At this point it's easy for some people to say, that it really is all about perseverance, and that everyone who got successful, had to go through a number of tries before they became wildly successful. Probably true, but then what is stopping us from trying again and again, till we are successful?

One of the things I have learnt is that whilst we may be intelligent, sensitive and smart, and may have what it takes to be somewhat successful, we tend to wither in the face of failure, rejection, criticism, etc. And we tend to wither fast. The same intelligence and sensitivity that got us to where we are, is now working against us. We have been used to being moderately successful in our own current line of work, and we have forgotten how to fail at things. We have forgotten that it will take a number of attempts before we become successful at something that is new to us. Or even if it is not new to us, it will take us a little more time before we become wildly successful.

Translated into simple terms. We are not willing to take "Multiple Plunges" into the unknown or known space, whilst handling failure.

Let me give you an example of a baby. When a baby wants something, it does not give up, pretty much till it gets what it wants. Else, it will fall asleep crying. But whenever it wakes up and remembers what it wants, it will let you know. And you will give it.

That's what we need to be doing, when we take the plunge. Plunge into whatever it is you want to do, again and again. You will fail, but you need to learn from your failure and plunge in again. Keep doing it. There will come a point when you will begin to enjoy it.

Let me ask you to do something. It is easy to do, but it will illustrate a very simple point.

Fold both your hands together the way it is shown below.

Once you have done the above, please check which of your thumb is on top. Is it the left one or is it the right one? Remember which ever one it is.

Now unfold both hands and put them back together again, making sure that this time you have kept the opposite thumb on top.

Feels a little awkward? Right?

What I can guarantee you, is that if you practiced this thing, by using the opposite thumb, for 21 days, then the next time you were doing it, the opposite thumb would be on top, and it would hardly feel awkward. That is the power of practicing something to make it a habit.

Repeatedly plunging in, to do what you want, has to become a habit.

It does not matter whether your first attempt is successful or not, it does not matter whether your 10th attempt is successful or not, you have to keep plunging in. You have to tell yourself it does not matter. Keep doing it for two reasons. One is because you like/love doing it. Two is because plunging back into doing it, has now become a habit.

I am going to spend a little more time here, because if you are still reading this, if you are one of those 0.01% who started out with this book and are still reading it, then I want to reiterate that this is probably the most important part of being successful.

Go back and do what you love doing. Go back and try it again, regardless of the number of times you have failed in the past. It is one of the proven paths to being wildly successful. The thing here is, you do need to love the thing you are doing. When I say love, I mean you need to really like doing that thing. If it's painting, you need to like or love the time that you spend doing that. If it's investing, you need to like it. If it's history or politics or adventure sports or golfing, whatever it is, you need to like doing it. It needs to give you enjoyment. At some point even doing what we love doing, will seem tedious, but at the end of it, it needs to give you a sense of achievement.

As you keep doing this, you will also realize you may need to change the angle of your plunge. What do I mean by that?

Whilst we need to keep plunging back in, we need to work towards doing it better and better. Each time we have made an effort we need to learn from it. Then we need to improve upon it.

Many years ago, I used to do theatre. It wasn't great. It was amateur theatre, but by God, I loved doing it. I wrote three or four plays, before one of them got a certain measure of success. I then took that one and did it three times, in two different cities, whilst trying out different production models, and finally by the last one, I made some money out of it. Every time I did one, I learned something, and I built on that for the next one. As I collaborated with people, newer ideas came about and I was able to alter the angle of my plunging in, which in the end, led to a better result.

If you love investing in stocks, if you love sports, if you love collecting antiques, if you love cooking, if you love restoring cars, if you love hiking, you are constantly learning as you keep doing it. You keep altering your approach to the same thing, as you learn newer things in your chosen field.

But then here comes the question again. Yes, I have learnt how to do what I like better, but I am not wildly successful yet! What do I need to do to become successful beyond my wildest dreams!

Here is where you need to find a way to make your passion work for you. Till now you have approached your passion, in a certain way. Can you think of doing it in a different way? In a way that allows you to indulge your passion, yet it makes you money and it makes you famous if that is what you want.

I will share a small example of how I did this on a very small scale. Again, it was not earth shattering, but it was a start.

Originally, I used to do plays, by funding it myself, either through spending money, or getting a few sponsorships. We would make some money from ticket sales, but it was never enough. I was about to stop doing plays all together, since they never really made money. But then I go an idea.

I had realized that the actors that we usually chose to do our plays, did it for free, since they were amateurs and they did it both for the love of doing these plays, but also for the exposure it gave them. They knew when the play was ultimately performed at a theatre, they would get some level of exposure.

As time went by, and I teamed up with a savvier producer, we realized that upcoming actors would be willing to pay us for a chance to be part of our production. The only guarantee we would give them, would be that they would get a chance to perform on stage at a reputable theater. My plays were usually written with 10 to 12 characters in mind. Once you stage a play you do at least 2 to 4 shows. What it meant is we could get about 24 people to sign on, on the understanding they would get two shows each, and we would have two groups practicing the same play at the same time. Since this was in Mumbai, India, we collected Rs.10,000, from each of the participants, which netted us about Rs. 240,000/-. Many years ago, this was a good sum of money which allowed us to cover production costs. Then depending on ticket sales etc. there was a chance we would break even or perhaps even make some money.

The point was I had cracked the code to doing what I loved, and making some bit of money from it. It was not a lot, but at least I wasn't spending my own money anymore!

The thing is, you need to figure out a way to see how you can use your passion to make money for you.

I know it's easier said than done. It's also not a new idea. Countless people are already trying this on You Tube, Tik Tok. Instagram and whatever else is out there. And a lot of them are becoming successful, but then a lot aren't as well.

I am one of those who aren't, at least till now. That is why you have probably not heard of me. And yet I am still writing. I am still taking the plunge over and over again, knowing deep down, that at some point, I will break through.

That is the belief you need to have. And that brings me to the next chapter.

But before I go there, it's important for me to check with you if you agree with me about plunging in. If you don't then I guess we are at two ends of the spectrum. I would like to hear from you about why you don't agree, and I am happy to listen to you and understand why you disagree. I am approachable and I will wait for you to contact me if you so desire.

If, however, you do agree with me, then here is a tip. There is probably something you do every day, something like brushing your teeth, or drinking water, or taking a particular medication. It probably takes you a few minutes, but you do find time for it every day. In the same way you need to find time for your passion for at least a minute every day, even if it's only to just think about it. (I am aware you can't start painting on canvas, if you are taking an international flight! But you can still think about it. So do it!) And when you are at home even if it is for a few minutes go and stand in front of your painting, or go and look at your real estate portfolio, or look up your favorite place to go.

The point is keep going back to what you need to do, everyday!

That's what plunging in is about. You have one life! Don't hold back. What you will find on the other side will change your life.

***

Path 3

Believe In Yourself

I often find myself doubting my capabilities. Gone are those days when as a kid, or as a teenager, I thought I could do anything, be good at anything. As time has passed by, I seem to have mellowed down.

But then again, once in a while I get this feeling, I am still good at what I like doing! I suddenly get that urge again to start believing in myself. And in some way, it helps me move forward in what I want to do.

What it made me realize is the need for us to believe in ourselves. Time for me to digress again!

Have you ever looked at someone doing something, someone reasonably famous, and then wondered, that you could do what they are doing much better? Has it ever happened to you? I can sense the answer is probably yes for some of us.

It is at that point that you think, "what if I had gone ahead and done what I had loved doing in the first place?" Admittedly there is more to this than just this level of wishful thinking.

People, whom we deem as successful, have usually not got their success by accident. They have probably worked hard and long to get to where they have got to. They have had to overcome obstacles, face losses and failures, faced disappointments and setbacks, before they reached a level of success. They have persevered in the face of various challenges, and most importantly they never gave up.

The question is how did they do it? How could they keep going, even when everything seemed like it was going against them?

The answer is "They believed in themselves."

Somewhere deep down, they had this innate belief in themselves, that they would be able to achieve their dream. They believed in their ability. They believed in their love for what they were doing. They believed in the World. They believed in themselves!

And that "belief in ourselves" is what we need to find, albeit, it may seem like we are a little late to the table.

What exactly do I mean by that?

What I mean is it's never too late to start. We may think our days of taking a stab at something we love doing are over. We may think our shot at being insanely successful is over. But the truth is, it's not. It never is.

But you have probably heard this before, right?

And yet here you are reading this same thing again, in a slightly different format.

<u>So, what exactly is holding you back?</u>

What holds us back is our lack of self- belief coupled with a sense of modesty, a sense that whilst we may be good at something, maybe we are not *that* good. This, along with the fact we often have an alternate job or profession to fall back on, does not help things.

But let's get back to "believing in oneself." How do we build this up within ourselves. How do we believe in ourselves to the extent, that we become so confident in our ability to do what we want to do, that nothing can ever stand our way. How do we do it?

We do it by explaining the following to ourselves.

Whatever it is I do, I am the only one who can do that thing in that particular way. And there is always a market for that.

It's true. There are millions of people who write. But what I write is my own. (Soon ChatGPT or AI will take over, but we are still a little bit away from that!). What I write, I do so in my own unique way. It may not be better than a lot of writers out there. It may not be wholly original. It may not be remarkable, but it is very definitely mine. And if you are the one last person still reading this, then I have made my point. There is at least a one-person market for what I do!

We, often undersell ourselves. (When I say, "we," I mean us, the "Neither Average, Nor Successful" group. As you recall, each one of you are above average. Each one of you is doing relatively well in life.)

However, we often undersell our own talents, to ourselves. We think what we have is good, but not good enough. And yet when you see someone doing that very thing you do, and being successful at it, you wonder, why it is not you, who is up there doing that thing. It's a very strange yet wistful feeling, and yet for us it's very strong. Most of the times we also have nobody to discuss it with. It's a feeling we may never even discuss with our closest ones.

The problem is, we are not going to wake up one day and start believing in ourselves. If you have not done it for so long, my writing about it and your reading it this once, is not going to change that. So, we need to think about how do we practically get there, over the next few weeks or months or years. Yes, for some of us this will take some time. Did you really think it would happen fast, when you picked up this book?

Let's assume that what you like doing is stock trading. Let's assume you are doing it well, making a 12 to 15% return, or sometimes even a 20% return. But then you are still not Jim Cramer. Even if you make a 35% percent return once in a while, you are still not Jim Cramer. You are not wildly successful yet. So how do you get there?

Let's assume you like singing or rapping. But you are not an Ed Sheeran or a John Harlow. How do you get there?

It's also not necessary to reach that level of success, but are we even at that next level from where we currently are? And if not, how do we get there?

You get there by convincing yourself that you are as unique as anyone, and that you can do it. You can achieve any level of success, once you set your mind on it. Once you believe in yourself. You don't have to be a Jim Cramer, or an Ed Sheeran, or anyone else for that matter. You want to be "You," but you want to be successful like them. And you have it within you to do that. You just need to believe it.

I am going to ask you to do something now. Try it.

Try smiling. Force a smile on your face and hold it for a bit. Keep holding it even it feels a little artificial. After a little while there is a likelihood, you find yourself actually smiling. Even if you don't, you feel a little twinge, a slight remembrance, of something nice.

We normally smile or laugh when we feel good or happy about something. It is a result of us feeling happy or good. However, when we force ourselves to simulate the result, there is a slight association with the cause, which gets triggered, which in this case is the feeling of happiness.

Similarly, were you to be as famous as one of the people you admire, what do you think would be happening? Would you be getting interviewed? Would you be getting photographed? Would people be trying to connect with you to get your advice? Would there be magazines or articles writing about you? Some of you may not want to be in the public gaze. You may want to be successful, but away from all the limelight. You would still be doing something differently, to what you are doing today.

What you need to do is try and imagine that. Try and live that feeling.

Get a nice photograph of yourself on top of a magazine and put it up somewhere, where you can see it every day. Imagine yourself being insanely successful. Think about it every day, and it will help you get there.

Imagine you are getting interviewed by someone. Think about what questions they may ask you and how you will answer them. Think about how you will tell them about your journey to success, tell them about what you did to get there. Tell them about the hours you spent working away, part time, at your passion, and how you got to where have now.

As you imagine yourself doing all the above, you will be doing two things.

One, you will be inspiring yourself. You will start believing in yourself. You will start attracting what you are imagining to yourself.

Two, you will also be telling yourself about the actual path you need to follow to be successful. Then go do it.

Imagine it, believe in it and then Do it!

Imagine it, **believe** in it and then **Do it!**

I call it the **IBD** method.

Some of you may be convinced about this method. But I do sense skepticism from quite a few of you. I welcome it. It is understandable.

Whether this works or not, will only be proven once you have tried it out for about a month. If you reject the idea, finish this book, and never try out this approach, then it will obviously not work. It will also not work if you try it half-heartedly.

For this to work you have to throw yourself into it whole heartedly, and with a belief that it will work. To the extent you are able to do this, you will be successful. That I am sure of. But you have to try it.

As a caveat, I do want to mention that this whole IBD thing only works for positive things. It does not work for something that is illegal, or something that involves hurting someone else, or taking something from someone else. Sometimes, on the outside, it may seem like it is working for some people, but in reality, it is not. Whilst it may seem that a lot of people are doing things that seem wrong, and yet they are having a good time doing that, they are not. We never really know the whole story, and so whatever things seem like, that is never the whole truth. And even if it is for a short while, things always have a way of catching up with you.

The point is, whatever you do, *it always has to be on the right side of the moral spectrum.*

One of the things, I can guarantee you, is that if there is something you want, if there is something you want to see, if there is something you want to manifest, then if you think about it long enough, if you believe in it enough, then one day you will find it. I will share an example below of something I found, something quite inconsequential in the big scheme of things, but nevertheless, meaningful to me.

I grew up in a couple of small dusty towns named Dhanbad and Ranchi, in what was called the State of Bihar, in India. In the 70s and 80s they were famous for coal mines and waterfalls. I grew up alongside coal miners' kids, played in the dusty lanes of Dhanbad, traded the choicest of abuses, got beaten up, ran away from home on my cycle, went to school, played cricket, and had a gala time! It was a vastly different World all together, from the World I live in today.

However, I used to read a lot, and there was one western author in particular whom I read a lot. We used to take a lot of train journeys in those days as well, to visit relatives, and in an era where there were no mobile phones or social media, reading was a form of escape. This particular author used to write voluminously, and for me the thicker the book, the more the bang for my buck. It also helped that he was a fantastic writer, at least for me. He was Stephen King!

I read a lot of his books, Two, things I used to wonder about when I read his books. The first was the storm/sewer drain that Georgie disappears down in the novel IT. I had no idea that a sewer drain opening looked like that. (The reason is it didn't where I was at that time.) But for some reason a picture of that storm/sewer drain remained in my mind. It was something that intrigued me. The other thing that intrigued me was when I read about a "black suburban" that was prowling around the neighborhood, again in one of his books. (I think it was called the "Regulators") I had never seen a black suburban as a kid.

More than 30 years later, I now live in a house where if I look out from my study, I can see the exact same Storm/Sewer drain opening, that Pennywise the clown inhabited in the novel. I also see a black Suburban almost every other day, given I now live in the US and travel around all the time.

Both of the above examples, are inconsequential, in the big scheme of things, but they were both something I had wanted to see. Somehow, I had the quiet belief that one day, I would figure it out, that one day, I would see these things and all my childhood wonder would flood back to me. And it did.

And that is the power of belief. The power of wanting something.

If you believe in something, if you want something, you will find it.

Sometimes, you need to sit back, close your eyes and just think about what you really want. What is it that you have always really wanted to do? Perhaps you already know it. And that is fantastic. If you don't, then sit and think, and you will find out. Calm your mind of the daily clutter, and think about what makes you happy. Really happy. And you will find it. And when you do, all you need to do is believe in your ability to attain it.

Sometimes, we will face a bit of self-doubt. That is natural. Almost every one you know who is successful has been plagued by the same. The only difference is they got past that.

One of the things with self-belief is that a lot of people around you, whether intentionally or unintentionally, will say things that will seem to erode your self-belief. That is something you will need to guard against. I bring it up because, a simple discouraging statement from someone around you about your capabilities, can often throw you back into your shell, from which it is very difficult to come out.

Let me give you an example. I think I am able to communicate reasonably well. I know I can. And yet one of my very well-meaning Supervisor in the Corporate World chose to give me feedback saying I needed to work on my communication with Senior Management. Mind you this was regarding an isolated incident, where, I did not have the full information, the time to craft a response, and she did not get the context. However, it suddenly seemed like I needed to work on my communication. Mind you this is the same supervisor who uses me for all their corporate events where I conduct workshops and group exercises which everyone loves.

Did I let that feedback define me or stop me? Obviously not, since here I am communicating with you and whoever else is reading this. But what it made me realize that we are often given some feedback in life, which can be detrimental to us depending on how we are able to navigate our response to the same. I have moved around a lot, been on both sides of the table, and have the ability to discern some of this feedback now. But I do realize that for some of us, it may actually stop us from pursuing what we think we are good at! And that would be an immense loss, not just to you, but to humanity at large!

I know for a fact that all of us have been in a similar situation. So, my call out to you is, forget what people have said to you, about your capabilities. Forget about your hesitation. Just go forth and do that thing, that you love. That you think you are good at!

It's a lot like Karaoke after a few drinks. 😊 I sometimes would happily kill the person, ruining a perfectly wonderful song! But then I think, the real point here is that person is enjoying themself, and that is all that matters!

So, coming back to my original point. Believe in yourself. Believe in your ability to do what you think you are good at and do it. A good way to push yourself to do it is this. You do only live once. As of now you only have a maximum of 40 to 90 years left to live, in a Universe that is billions of years old. So why not try out what you truly love? What have you got to lose, by believing in yourself?

The answer is nothing!

So, believe in yourself and plunge into what you love doing. I can guarantee you will come out the other side!

Path 4

Follow on and feel your way through

We often make a good start. We feel encouraged and enthused to set off on our journey to being successful! And that is indeed the way it should be.

But then after a few days, or few weeks, or even a few months, we tend to start flagging. It happens a little at first, and then maybe a little more, and then soon we have hung up our gloves, and have gone back to our routine.

I think you know what I am talking about.

How do we keep going on with what we have set out to do, especially if we are not seeing the results of the same? We may have started off with something, it's working a little bit, but it's not really taking off. We may have made some investments, but they have not taken off. We may have started painting, but have not finished what we started. We may have started carving that beautiful piece of furniture, but for some reason am unable to complete it. We made about 30 You Tube videos, but then stopped.

Here is where you need to learn how to keep following on and feeling your way through the journey you have chosen to undertake. It's ploughing through with what you have started. It may seem like a chore, but you need to make it happen. It's that time where you need to push yourself a little, knowing deep down, that this push is what you need to take you to the other side. To take you from being above average to wildly successful!

There will come a time, and it happens to everyone, where you question what you are doing. Where you think, your efforts are not getting you anywhere. The key is to not stop. You need to keep following on. This does not mean though, that you keep doing what you have been doing blindly.

It's perfectly normal to make course corrections to what you have been doing. For example, you may realize there is a different way to do what you are doing. Or you realize there is one aspect of what you are doing that is resulting in greater success. It may make sense to focus on that aspect of your initiative. We will talk more about that in the next chapter where we deal with changing and experimenting. For now, we will focus on how you keep following through with what you have started on.

This is where you begin to feel your way through the intricacies of how you can be successful!

You, are an intelligent person. You are already above average. We established that at the beginning of this book. So, by that logic, if you find yourself stuck with whatever it is you are doing, it is not going to be very difficult for you to figure out why you are not making progress.

If you just sit down and think about what you are doing, you will soon realize there are a few different ways in which you can take things forward. For example, if you have started a food business, and it is not taking off, then there could be several reasons. Either the food is not being made well. Or people don't know about your Business. Or you have a location problem. Or you have priced it too high. There could be a number of reasons and if you sit down and analyze things you will soon figure out what needs to be done. At that point you go make the change and then wait for the results. If for some reason the first thing you do, does not have an impact, then try something else. It's a process that you have to convince yourself to follow.

The answers will always be out there. It's up to us to keep following through. And this is the most difficult part of being successful.

Of all the things that I have mentioned above, this part is the most crucial. If you are able to break through this part, you are pretty much assured of success! If you have read on till now, if you have started off on your journey to be wildly successful, then this is where you have to concentrate on the most.

The bad news:

This is the most difficult part.

The good news:

9 out of 10 people, who are reading this book, will probably give up at this stage. And that means you have moved into that 10% of people who have a shot at being wildly successful.

If you are able to push yourself through this phase, success is likely coming your way. You will realize that when you find you are forcing yourself back to your dream endeavor, over and over again. Whether it is trading, athletics, media, writing, building, developing, designing, cooking, setting up a business, singing, dancing, politics, or anything you are pursuing in order to move towards success.

One of the ways you are able to do this, is by having chosen something, that gives you a certain amount of joy. That is why it's important to try and do something you like doing. We said that at the beginning of this book.

You may not like every aspect of the overall business that will make you successful, but at least if it is centered on something fundamental you love doing, then there is chance you will be able to pull through on that front. An important thing to remind you about here is, don't hesitate to ask for help.

Or even better, if you can afford it go and hire someone who can help you with the parts of your endeavor that you are NOT good at.

For example, I may love writing, but editing is not my strong point. I can easily get someone else to do that for me, which frees me up to concentrate on writing.

It's therefore important to feel your way through whatever it is you are doing and continue to make changes and tweaks as needed.

As I mentioned earlier following through is the most crucial aspect of becoming successful! I have been writing stuff for about 25 years, without much to show for it! And yet I keep following through!

One of the things about doing this which I think is a game changer is trusting your feelings or instincts about what you are doing! It will sound strange, but we all get a feeling about what we are doing. The feeling can be about a number of things. It could be a feeling about whether our idea is good or not, whether we are going in the right direction or not! Are we doing something that will be liked by people? Are we doing something that is scalable or not.

Deep down we have an idea that we think will be successful. We feel it in our bones! We know! And yet we often doubt ourselves. Or we get swayed by people, who are quick to point out, that your idea may not have feet, in terms of making money. And often times we give up.

Learn to trust your feelings or instincts. If you feel that your idea or venture or endeavor has a chance of success, then follow that feeling.

There is probably a path out there that is known only to you, and if you stick to it long enough you will find it. It takes belief in yourself and it takes the courage to keep following through.

When I was writing this book, I had doubts about who would read this. There are millions of self-help books out there. Why would people read this one? How would they even know about it? Moreover, this was aimed at a niche audience of people who were above average and only wanted to be more successful. It was probably a small number to start with. So, should I even go forward with this?

And here is what is important. Really important. I just had this feeling that somehow there was a market for exactly this kind of a book. Somehow, I felt there were a lot more people out there, who were struggling with this concept. And that they needed something that talked about it. Or at least touched upon the subject. There was no data that I had to support this feeling. No data at all! And yet I had this strong feeling it would work. And if you have been reading up to this point, you know it has, at least to a certain extent. At least for one person.

The point is if we are feeling something, there is a very strong reason we are feeling that. It is the unexplainable part of being successful. And it is crucially important we are able to discern which feeling we are experiencing the most strongly and which feeling we think we are going to follow. It is like an inbuilt compass and we need to follow it.

It's similar to trusting your instincts in a way. It is the universe trying to tell you something. Don't ignore it, especially don't ignore it because someone made some trivial remark about how your idea may not work! No one else understands where you are really coming from. Only you can. And if you follow through you may just be the one who changes things in this World!

It is important to validate your feelings, and you are the only one who can do that. One of things about a feeling that you should heed, is that it keeps coming back to you. It pops up in your mind, not just once, but multiple times. It goes away for some time, but it always keeps coming back to you. That is an easy way of identifying a feeling you have about an idea that is strong, and that has a chance of success.

One of the things you have to remember is there is space in this Universe for every idea. Even ideas that have been tried and tested. Some simple examples are Restaurants or Beauty Salons or music albums. They are not new ideas in themselves, but you have thousands of new restaurants and beauty Salons opening up every year. You have people making new albums every year and some of them become big successes! It's because someone believed that they could execute that generic idea in a different way and be successful. Take the concept of Franchising. It is someone else's idea that you like that you will be executing on. However, your passion and dedication and effort that you put in will define the success of that venture. How you feel about it and how you feel your way through the process will define your success!

The bottom line here is to keep going and keep trusting your own feelings!

Path 5

Keep Changing & Experimenting

One of things you have to believe by now, is that you are on your way to being wildly successful! If you have been reading with attention, if you have been doing the exercises that were suggested earlier on, then you well and truly are, on a path to success!

You have identified what you like and you have your sentence ready, somewhat like what is shown below:

I am *(insert whatever it is you want),* ***in the most wonderful manner. I am in perfect health. I am able to talk about my*** *(insert whatever it is you want)* ***and share it with the World. I am famous and well known.***

Some of you may not want to be famous or well known, in which case you just delete the last line.

So now you have already embarked on your journey!

Some of you may not have done any of the exercises and have just been reading through. And I thank you for that. If you have got so far, then all I can assure you is that if you go back and read through this book again, if you do the exercises that have been outlined, then you will be on your path to success. All you need to do is take action!

Now, it's likely you may have forgotten what I wrote about earlier, so I will recap a little below:

Let's assume you have identified what you want and have got a sentence written out. You have then found some level of appreciation for what you want, either from someone around you, or from yourself! Then you have taken the plunge and started on whatever it is that you wanted to do. You now believe in yourself and your idea, and you are following it and feeling your way through to success!

The final thing that you need to be able to do is to *keep changing and experimenting* as needed.

No idea is a perfect idea the first time. Even the biggest of firms keep changing and tweaking and modifying their strategy, their product and their offerings. And you need to be able to that. The fancy corporate word for it is to be able to "pivot." (Mind you there is a lot of pivoting that goes on in the Corporate World that makes no sense, but the concept in itself is sound!)

Whatever your idea is, you need to plunge in and test it out. As you learn more about it you need to be open to changing it, or experimenting with it. Is it working? Are people liking it? Are you liking it? Is it making sense? Etc.

There are numerous articles on how to do this, how to identify your target market, how to relentlessly focus on the end user etc. etc., but the point is you will know what to look for and when you are able to identify a need to change, just do it. Feel free to experiment, and something will click and you will have your Billion Dollar gig!

I will share with you something I have experienced first-hand. But before I go there, I will back up for a second.

You may have noticed I did not share stories and examples of people who are already famous through their hard work or through following a version of what I have outlined above. The reason I did not do that, is because 1) you have probably already heard of how they did it, 2) hearing about them does not really help you!

You need to hear about how a nobody or someone like myself struggled to get where I have got to, where I have done all the above and who now believes they have a shot at that Billion Dollar idea! And all that is standing between this nobody and success, is the time it takes to make the changes and carry out the experiments that will be needed.

If you are ready to go on that journey with me, please carry on reading. Else you could skip to the end where all you need to do is Congratulate yourself on your success and share it with us!

I doubt you will stop reading at this stage, but if you do goodbye! I am impressed you made it this far!

For years I have been plagued with having ideas! I would always have these outlandish ideas, which I believed had a prominent place in this

World, but then I had no way of bringing it to people. I would write out my ideas, I would share them with Magazines, I would write some of them into Plays and get them performed. But at the end of the day, it never got beyond a few thousand people. The only thing that still kept me going, was I believed in my ideas, and my writing and my productions. I often saw lesser ideas, or lesser innovations being far more successful, whatever the reason. But it never totally killed my belief in myself. In some of the darker moments, I did think that my ideas weren't good enough, or that I wasn't trying hard enough, but somehow, I don't think I ever gave up.

Years went by. I got caught up in the Corporate World which paid my bills, but I could never shake off that side of me that wanted something more. The side of me that wanted to be Wildly Successful!

I wrote a book about "How to get Married" and it got published! I acted in small parts in a couple of movies! I produced and directed plays! And, yet nothing really happened. I kept getting pushed back into the Corporate Grind, which paid my bills and gave me a moderately decent lifestyle, but not the success I really wanted.

So, I kept pushing. I kept writing. I kept coming up with ideas. But then without having anyone to share them with they all amounted to nothing!

What was I to do?

How was I going to break through this status quo? And mind you I am not talking days or months here; I am talking years!

I have had ideas around many topics a few of which are outlined here. The reason I do so is I am sure a lot of you have had similar ideas or thoughts. You may even have done something about some of them to a certain extent, but then they are still lying around, as is the case with me, with no real traction in the real World! The bottom line is it has not made us wildly successful.... yet!!

One of my earliest ideas was a story around how predictions that happen in the Eastern World could define the Global Future. In most Eastern cultures there are predictions that people can make based on time of birth, astrological charts and other such things. Whilst a lot of it has been dismissed as speculation, no one has really tried to test the theory. My story was set in a World where a Global Corporation was trying to test out the validity of Astrological Predictions.

The reason a Global Corporation would invest in such an enterprise, would be profit. The question was where would they see profit in a venture like this? The answer was simple. If things and events could be predicted, even with 90% accuracy, imagine what it would mean for someone with that type of information? Imagine, how that type of information would impact the Stock Markets globally? It would be a game changer, and the people who would have this information would be Billionaires.

So, in my story this Global Corporation sets about establishing a way to test their theory. As they went about it, they realized they needed a test parameter they could easily measure. A parameter they could easily detect and measure globally. Unfortunately, the parameter they pick is death! And there is a good reason for that.

The death of a person is one of the things that Astrological predictions can pick up. It is also an easy thing to track in most Countries. So, it made the cut, in terms of being the element of measure. What the Corporation then did, is put together a few hundred of the best Astrologers they could find. They then picked a sample of 1 million People across the World and asked these Astrologers to do just one thing. Predict the time of their death.

(I know this sounds depressing, but remember it's just a story, I am talking about here!)

The story, which I had named "The Prediction" started out with a person getting involved in a car accident, and then miraculously surviving! Turns out she was supposed to die, and the Global Corporation who was tracking her astrologically predicted death, terms her as an "exception" and sends in someone to investigate.

As the investigation unfolds it turns out that whilst this lady is a true exception, her being so poses a threat to the theory that some people are trying to prove. Which is "That Astrological Predictions Work."

Given that a lot is riding on both the outcomes of this experiment, it turns out that there is a group of people who are now trying to kill the "exception!"

And there you have it! Enough of a story to create a block buster action movie. I actually wrote it as a short story, and it's still lying around gathering dust. (i.e. if a computer file can gather dust!)

The point is, it was a fresh idea. It still is. But I have never been able to do anything with it. The few people I have shared it with have always said it's a great idea. But that's where it's remained.

I have shared below a very small extract of what I had written then, to give you a flavor how I saw it playing out as a possible movie.

Astro Research had the un-enviable task of tracking the deaths of one million chosen subjects all around the World. 100 accomplished Astrologers had been chosen for this mammoth task of predicting just one aspect with accuracy, the exact time and place of death of each of these one million subjects.

Each of these death predictions was based on the exact time and place of the subject's birth. The means for gathering this data was a daunting task. More so were to set the parameters for monitoring the accuracy of the predictions. However, through a complicated system of data mining Astro Research had reduced all this to a series of screens which monitored each life like a sort of ECG graph which kept on moving across the screen towards its final date which had been predicted and fed into the system. A red line usually appeared on the screen signifying the time of a particular subject's death. It usually appeared about 12 hours before the subject was supposed to die. The agonizing part for most of the monitoring staff was to watch the last twelve hours of the subject's green lifeline move towards the red line. When the green line reached the red line and the incident claiming the subject's life took place the green line would mushroom out and merge into the red line signifying death.

Sometimes the green line would cross the red line and there would be a first level exception. At this point a blue line would appear at the far end of the screen signifying a time bandwidth of 13 hours and 30 minutes. This was the grace time given for the prediction to come true since a certain tolerance was built into such predictions. 99% of the first level predictions never went beyond 6 hours and only a 0.1% had ever crossed this blue line to qualify as a true exception.

Even all this sophisticated monitoring had its problems and mistaken data entry was one of the single major causes for these exceptions. Stringent measures had been adopted for correct data entry around the world and each particular place and time of birth of an individual was cross checked at least 7 times through 4 different data collection Agencies which had been set up for this very purpose. Three other Astrologers, crosschecked every prediction made by one Astrologer unknown to him or her. Only after all this data was verified was a subject put onto the system.

Kryshelin had often found herself looking at a green line jerking its way towards the red line and hoping that it would cross it. She would follow the ones, which had crossed over for the blue with even more eagerness. She used to find herself disappointed and empty as the blue line caught most of the hopefuls. She always seemed to find herself wishing that the green line would cross the blue line and somehow prove the prediction wrong.

One of my other ideas, was around Sleeplessness!

This revolved around the concept that the Human race did not need to sleep. Yes, yes, I know it sounds a little far-fetched, but if you have ever watched a Vampire Movie or a horror movie or even a Super Hero movie, then you need to give me some leeway!

My theory was, and this is true, that we have still not been able to prove why exactly people sleep. I know we talk about rest etc., but did you know that till now, scientists still don't know the exact reason for why we need to sleep.

The longest a person has gone without sleep has been 11 days, and whilst the person was somewhat disoriented there was no material damage to his health.

Anyway, given this was a science fiction cum fantasy, my theory, in the story, was that sleep was a disease. It was a virus that caused us to sleep, so they could feed on us whilst we slept.

That formed the backdrop of the adventure. I made the virus appear like a negative copy of every human, since it fed on a particular human, whilst they slept, and slithered away in the morning. But were they to be seen they would appear as a negative version of yourself!

Sounds outlandish, but it's the perfect fodder for a movie, in that particular genre!

The above are story ideas, and I had about a dozen of those, but I promise not to bore you with those.

The thing is I keep getting plagued with ideas in other spheres as well.

I get ideas about Real Estate, I get ideas about Human Longevity, I get ideas about wearable robotics and how it will revolutionize our World, I get ideas about how the dynamics of human interaction will change as robots become more commonplace and so on.

The point is I keep getting these ideas, I keep mulling over them for some time and then I move onto something else. As I mentioned earlier, I took some to fruition, some I discarded, and some I just forgot about.

The only thing I did consistently was to keep changing and experimenting with more and more ideas. Ideas for stories, Ideas in general and Ideas for Business.

I have finally come up with my Billion Dollar idea, which I know will in some shape or form change the World and probably make me somewhat successful. I will talk about that idea a little later. The point I want to make is this.

Keep changing and keep experimenting.

Even this latest idea of mine, will go through a lot of change. I am sure of that. How exactly it will turn out is anybody's guess. But if I keep going at it, I know it will reach somewhere. And this time, I know enough not to give up. Not to stop midway, but to keep going till the very end.

There will be a lot of people who will tell you what to do. Listen to people, they will usually have good advice, but ultimately it is you and your conviction that will take you through. That is all there is to it. Believe in your idea and it will find a way to blaze through. Sometimes it will not quite work the way you envision it. And sometimes that is what people term as failure.I term it as the opportunity to change tracks and experiment. Try the same idea a little differently, or try a variation of it, or try something the very opposite of what the original idea was and it might work! Be open to changing and experimenting and you will find success!

None of the success stories you hear about have been simple straight lines. They have all been through this process and whilst they do talk about it, it's not the part that we give a lot of attention to. And in a lot of cases this is the most important part of being wildly successful.

I will now talk a little bit about my idea. But again, feel free to skip and go to the end of the book, should you so desire.

My idea is simple. It's a website for a normal middle-class person with a family to connect meaningfully. It could be called something like Famly.com, or Married.Com, or MiddleClass.com. (I am still figuring it out!) I know there are millions of websites out there. But if you look carefully, there really is nothing, on a large scale for families to connect. You have famous websites for friends. You have big websites for jobs. You have websites for dating. You have websites for Finance, you have websites for just about everything, but you don't have a website that focuses on a normal family.

There is no website that a couple or a family could join to exchange views, thoughts and concerns about everyday life. Currently they are doing it on some of the larger websites through groups, but then that is just a small slice of what a family needs.

A family needs a lot. Depending on what stage a family is at, starting from Marriage, to having children, to children growing up, to pets, to financial needs, to medical needs, to college decisions - the list is endless!

If you look at the top 10 websites today, they are great for connecting with friends, they are great for networking and looking for jobs. Some of them are great for hours of scrolling and viewing the World through the myriad landscape of different people and different thoughts and concepts. Then there are websites where you can comment and post things, where famous people share their thoughts and you get to further comment on the same.

But there is nothing on that scale that lets a middle-aged person, connect with another likeminded person and discuss for example, the challenges they are facing in financial planning and at the same time, the challenges they are facing at their child's school. Or conversely to share something that their children have done in a group that is composed of like-minded families. (As I said before, there are sub groups like this that have formed on some of the famous websites, but there is no single large website that brings this together.)

And that is what I am going to do.

I have **Imagined** it; I **believe** in it and I am in the process of **Doing** it!

If you recall I had called it the **IBD** method. **Imagine** it, **believe** in it and then **Do it! (IBD)**

It is both simple and hard at the same time. The idea I have is simple enough to articulate. Staying with it and building it out will require an enormous effort! It will require thought, investment, significant effort and with it will come setbacks and challenges as well. But all that can be managed. What is perhaps the most difficult to manage is the initial self-doubt. Will I be able to sustain it? Will I be able to adequately change and experiment with the idea? For example, is it too family focused? Will I need to make it broader based?

And then the real killer. Someone tells you all that you have thought of is already being fulfilled by XYZ.

You will face this with any idea. I have faced it and am still facing it. But what I keep thinking about is that Billion Dollar buy out that will happen once I reach critical mass. And so, I keep ploughing ahead. I keep **believing** in myself and I keep **doing** what I need to do!

That is all there really is to becoming Wildly Successful!

Plunge in and start. Do whatever it is you want to. You have one life. Make the most of it. That is why we are all here. To make the most of this life. To make it meaningful. To make it so exciting for yourself that you wake up every morning, trying to do the thing that makes you happy and wildly successful!

Ask yourself this question.

What is really holding you back? What is it really? Is it time? Is it money? Is it your health? Is it your family? Is it your current job? Is it that you lack the will?

Think long and hard, and you will find that the answer usually boils down to something different.

Procrastination.

All the above questions I asked can be addressed. Addressing procrastination is usually the hardest. When we are telling ourselves, that we will do it later, or we will do it when we have the time, or we will do it when we retire, we are in a way cheating ourselves.

There is no time like now. There is no time like the present.

In an online World like ours, there is practically nothing you cannot get done online. You can set up a company within hours. You can reach out to people immediately. You can order online stuff within a day! Some things may take a few days or weeks, or even months to do, but the point is, things can be done much faster these days than before. All we have to do is seize the opportunity!

We live in a World today where you can order AI to whip up a presentation in a matter of minutes. You can speak to anyone almost anywhere in the World on Video. You can send messages to anyone. You are reaping the benefits of advanced medical technologies, the types of which have not been seen before!

You are truly blessed!

In such an environment, all you need to do is take action. Take action on doing what you love! Take the plunge and you will see the results unfold in front of you within weeks and months, if not days!

It is indeed one of the best times in Human history to try your hand at doing something you have always wanted to do!

As you go ahead on your journey be ready to keep changing and keep experimenting. Try out new ways of doing what you wanted to do. Keep an open mind. You never know what immense opportunity is lying in wait for you and your idea just around the corner!

***

Congratulate Yourself!

It's time to congratulate yourself!

One for almost finishing the book! But more importantly for having taken the first step towards being wildly successful! If you did not believe in being wildly successful, you would not have stayed with me till here. And if you have, then you have already taken the first step in that direction. You know what to do.

You now need to do it.

At the same time, you also need to congratulate yourself every step of the way! It's something we often forget when we are slogging away at the very thing that will make us successful!

I have written a lot, done stuff on the side, which has brought me to this moment. But I realized on hindsight, that I never celebrated any of the small successes I had! I never congratulated myself on what I had done! Admittedly a lot of what I have done is gathering dust, but it was something I had done. Something that deserved my own appreciation!

And that is what we often fail to do. I don't want you to repeat the same mistake. If you do something, anything, that takes you a wee bit forward on your journey to being successful, learn to celebrate that. You deserve it, you need it!

People celebrate ground breaking ceremonies, people celebrate launches, but we keep our own little achievements guarded and under wraps. I understand being modest. I understand you may not want to reveal too much too early. I agree with that. But there comes a time, and you will know that within yourself, where you do need to celebrate your own achievements. Even if it is the fact that you have managed to think about your next idea.

You need to be the first one to congratulate yourself! Otherwise, nobody else will!

The reason I say this, is because you need it. You need the celebration! You need the appreciation, even if it is from yourself! That is what will fuel you through the hard parts. That is what will keep you going. For make no mistake it is a hard journey.

If you have ever watched a movie where the protagonist achieves something that is beyond the ordinary, you will notice how they portray that. The person keeps trying or training, or making all the necessary efforts, whilst there is a feel-good music that plays in the background. It shows how they keep trying in the face of failure, and then how they slowly manage to get better and better and then ultimately succeed. A lot of this happens within a few minutes in the film. You see it, you register it and you feel good about it. Especially with all the music blasting away in the background!

In real life there is no music. At least that's what I felt the most. It's the actual grind you have to go through. And that does not happen in minutes. It's hours, days, weeks and years! Hours of effort and dedication. Days of perseverance. Weeks of patience and months of slogging. And then one day you realize you have spent years on the stuff and you are yet to reach anywhere.

One of the reasons for this is we don't congratulate ourselves enough when we reach certain milestones, within this journey. We owe it to ourselves, because it will energize us for the rest of the journey.

Make sure you take a pause in your journey and congratulate yourself for what you have achieved so far. Give yourself the credit. Even you have just started that painting. Even if you have just thought about a good investment. Even if you have taken some baby steps in whatever it is that you want to do. Don't hold back. Because deep down your soul is craving for it. It needs it in order to keep going. In order for you to achieve all the success you desire!

At the end share your success with us ☺

And yes, this is the end of the book. It's the end of me writing on this subject for quite some time, if that's of any relief to you!

The only thing I do ask of you, is should you become insanely successful, please share your success with us. By us, I mean me and all the others who might have read this book.

It will serve as an inspiration to all of us. It will give us all hope. It will pave the way for more people to follow in your footsteps and possibly learn from your experience.

Some of you may end here and never read this book again and forget about it. Some of you may try to follow it and stop. A few of you may follow through further, and you will find yourself on the path to success. And finally, some of you will become successful. Not because of this book, but because it is what you really want. Because it is something that is as important to you as breathing. It is because deep down you have always known that you wanted to be a runaway success! And you always knew that somehow or other, at some time or the other, you would get there! And now you have!

And all I ask of you is to share that with everyone you can!

You can always share it with me at dreamsellers12@gmail.com.

The End

One last thing

Play to your strengths

We all have certain strengths.

When you are aiming to be wildly successful, you need to leverage your strengths to the maximum. Recognizing what your strengths are is an important part of your journey.

We usually know what our strengths are but it's also a good idea to talk to someone whom you trust to tell you what *they* think are your strengths. Sometimes you may be surprised at what others perceive your strengths to be.

Make a list of your strengths and then analyze them. You fill find there are some strengths that you know about. For example, I can remember characters in movies and books. (It may not be a very valuable strength, but I have it.) I don't need to make an effort to remember them, and it comes to me naturally.

Then there are some strengths you have that people might have told you about, but which don't come to you naturally. Again, for example, some people have told me I am meticulous, and that I can get into the detail. Now that is a strength, I have that I can call upon if needed, but it does not come to me naturally. Normally I am not into the details. Normally I am not meticulous.

It's important to know what your natural strengths are and what your acquired strengths are. They are both useful depending on the circumstances.

Then there are some things which people tend to term as weaknesses, but which I term as "areas you may not be really interested in." I will share an example. I am literally dyslexic when it comes to remembering roads and directions. I am dyslexic to the extent I have sometimes forgotten my way home.

There was a time when I would tell myself I needed to remember roads better, or that I needed to get better at reading maps etc. But as time went on, I realized it was just something that did not interest me. For some reason, I did not retain information on roads and directions. It's not something I have set out to do deliberately, but it just does not interest me, the way it does a lot of others. Luckily in today's World I can get away with it given google maps and the like.

So, coming back to your list of strengths, it's important you make a list of them, especially the ones that come to you naturally. There is a great likelihood you will find a connection between your natural strengths and the sentence you have chosen or written earlier on in the book.

If you are naturally good at numbers, investing in the stock market may be your thing. If you are naturally good at interacting with people and love socializing, then public service may be your chosen path. If you are mechanically inclined, restoring old cars may be something you could make career out of.

Even if your strengths don't align exactly with your passion, you will find you need to use them in taking your passion forward. You may have a natural flair for talking to people. That would help you in marketing or selling your idea when the time is right.

It's extremely important though to recognize your own strengths and then leverage them on your path to success. Your strengths are what will give you that edge. Your strengths in particular areas will help you navigate some of the hard parts of your journey.

Playing to one's strengths is usually a cornerstone for most successful people. It's what you are naturally good at, or naturally inclined to. It makes it easier.

A good recipe for success is where you capitalize on your strengths, and where you find other people to help you in the areas you are not interested in. For example, in my day job, my strengths are managing people and executing on projects. That is what I am good at and that is what I focus on. I am not great at financial analyses and I leverage other people on the team who are good at that. I am also not good at reading complicated agreements, and for those I leverage external lawyers.

Similarly, when you craft your plan for being successful, make sure you surround yourself with people, who complement your strengths. That way you will have the best of all Worlds. Never make the mistake of trying to develop strengths you clearly don't have. Not for something that is immediate and important.

That's the reason a lot of very successful people have managers or agents, because they realize their strengths generally lie in their field of expertise and that is what they focus on. They let their managers or agent take care of a number of other things, that they are probably better at.

In the short time that you have to become wildly successful, you don't want to spend a lot of time working on what you are not good at, or what does not interest you. You want to maximize your chances of success and that will happen only if you leverage the strengths, you already have.

Even games like American Football, Base Ball, Cricket etc., always leverage their players strengths and use them in positions where their greatest strengths lie.

It's all about getting the maximum benefit with what you already have.

***

BACK PAGE BLURB

In the unlikely event you have picked up this book, and you are part of the 650 million people in this World who are either on their way to achieving a net worth of $1 Million or are already there, then this book might be for you.

You are smart, you are above average, you are growing in life and you are leading a decent existence. You already know that. But you want something more!

You want to be more than just above average. You want to break through to other side, where you are wildly successful! So wildly successful that you yourself could not have imagined it, or perhaps did not dare imagine it before this.

Is it even possible? How do these people who are so wildly successful, so famous, how do they do that? Are they really very different from me? Haven't I been putting in a lot of the same hard work as they have? Was it luck, was it some help they had that I did not? Are they really much smarter than I am?

If somewhere deep down, you think you can be wildly successful, then this could be a book that gives you a few insights into an approach, that might possibly work.